Outstanding Praise for *Raising Your Child to Be a Champion in Athletics, Arts, and Academics:*

"This book can be read in an afternoon, but the positive effects will last a lifetime. The concepts seem so basic and yet we tend to forget them on a daily basis. Keep a yellow marker handy when you read this book; you wil̲ ̲ ̲light the secrets to a better life for everyone close to ̲ ̲ ̲ ̲ ̲"

—Vic Br̲ ̲ ̲ ̲ ̲ ̲ ̲ ̲ ̲ ̲ ̲ ̲ ̲ ̲ ̲ tennis coach,
Vis̲ ̲

"*Raising Your* ̲ ̲ ̲ ̲ ̲ ̲ ̲ ̲ ̲ ̲ ̲ ̲ ̲ ̲ ̲ ̲ personifies Wayne Bryan's enthusi̲ ̲ ̲ ̲ ̲ ̲ ̲ ̲ ̲ ̲or life. It presents simple, concise, short an̲ ̲ ̲ ̲ ̲ ̲ ̲ ̲ ̲ers full of relevant and fascinating anecdotes! ̲ ̲ ̲ ̲ ̲ ̲ ̲ ̲ ̲k is tremendously uplifting—it simply 'feels good!' ̲ ̲ ̲ ̲ecipe offered in *Raising Your Child to Be a Champion* really works. This must be one of the best and most useful books on 'parenting' ever written."

—Dick Gould, record-setting men's tennis
coach, Stanford University

"Since parenting is the most important profession . . . I urge all to read this book."

—John R. Wooden, head basketball coach
emeritus, UCLA

"This little book is great for Everybody. It will even help coaches, and you can believe that!"

—Sparky Anderson, Hall of Fame manager
for the Cincinnati Reds and Detroit Tigers

"I truly LOVE it! It was so refreshing to hear from a guy whose kids have succeeded at the highest levels."

—Lissa Muscatine, Hillary Clinton's
press secretary, Washington, D.C.

Raising Your Child to Be a Champion

in *A*thletics, *A*rts, and *A*cademics

WAYNE BRYAN

with Woody Woodburn

CITADEL PRESS
Kensington Publishing Corp.
www.kensingtonbooks.com

CITADEL PRESS BOOKS are published by

Kensington Publishing Corp.
850 Third Avenue
New York, NY 10022

All Kensington titles, imprints, and distributed lines are
available at special quantity discounts for bulk purchases for
sales promotions, premiums, fund-raising, educational, or
institutional use. Special book excerpts or customized printings
can also be created to fit specific needs. For details, write or
phone the office of the Kensington special sales manager:
Kensington Publishing Corp., 850 Third Avenue, New York, NY
10022, attn: Special Sales Department; phone 1-800-221-2647.

First printing: July 2004

10 9 8 7 6 5 4 3 2 1

Printed in the United States of America

CIP data is available.

ISBN 0-8065-2660-2

To Kathy, Mike and Bob
who have brought so much joy and inspiration
into my life, and to Carl and Alice, great parents and pals.

—Wayne Bryan

To Lisa, Dallas and Greg—you are my Formula
for happiness.

—Woody Woodburn

Acknowledgments

Special thanks to: Kathy Bryan who was so instrumental in the creation of this Formula and who is an excellent and dedicated editor.

And also thanks to: Steve Bellamy, Becky Blake, Lynn Grady, Steve Loft, Steve Pratt, Brad Simon and Mark Weil for their help with this project. Their comments and suggestions were invaluable.

Contents

Why and How I Created My Formula for Success

*F*or many, many years, people have asked me, "How did you do it? How did you raise your sons to be great tennis players, great students and also great *kids*?"

And then, before I can even try to give them an answer, they ask: "Can you tell me how to do it?"

It was these questions that inspired me to write down what my wife Kathy and I did while raising our twin sons, Mike and Bob, who are now both tennis professionals playing on the ATP Tour and who both won full-ride scholarships to Stanford University. Initially, I used the Formula we came up with in my speaking engagements across the country.

However, about five years ago I realized I had to do more. Following every single one of my lectures or clinics, numerous people would come up to me and ask if they could buy a book with my Formula for raising a champion. When I would reply I didn't have a book out, invariably they said I should hurry up and write one.

Well, now I finally have with the help of my good friend and national award-winning sports columnist

Woody Woodburn. Ideally, you will read this book from cover to cover and implement it in its entirety. In fact, *Raising Your Child to be a Champion in Athletics, Arts, and Academics* is like shampoo—for best results, repeat! Read it again and again. Refer back to it. Use more of it.

Each chapter represents a cornerstone of my Formula for Success, and if you follow the advice in just one of those chapters, your child will benefit. If you follow them all, it will be *great* for your child.

My Formula is not just a blueprint for raising your own child to be a champion in tennis, or any other sport or discipline, it is a blueprint for raising your child to be a champion student and a champion *person*. As you will discover in reading this book, I strongly believe these all go hand-in-hand. Excellence carries over in all facets of our lives.

Raising a child into an excellent person is the most important thing you can ever do as a parent. If you blow it, it will haunt you and cause problems—for you and your child-turned-adult—the rest of your lives. But if you do an excellent job, it will reward you both forever.

It is the most important thing we do, and yet we don't have much time to do it. We get *only* eighteen years to do so. Yes, I said only eighteen years, because believe me, that isn't very long.

A framed reminder of this concept of how fleeting the time I had with my boys has hung on my office wall since shortly after Mike and Bob were born. It reads:

Turn around and they're 2. Turn around and they're 4.
Turn around, they're a young man heading out the door.

I found this to be so very true. Mike and Bob hit their first tennis balls at age 2 on Monday, went to kindergarten on Tuesday, entered high school on Wednesday and graduated on Friday. At Stanford, they went up there on Monday and they were going out on the professional tennis tour after their sophomore years on Tuesday. It seems like an exaggeration but believe me, looking back, it isn't. Your time with your children as children is unbelievably fleeting.

The eighteen years you have to raise your child are also priceless. I was reminded of this at an ATP Tour junior tennis clinic held in Ponte Vedra, Florida, in 1995. My driver to the airport after the event was a wise and charismatic older gentleman named George Soper.

During our ride and conversation, I learned that besides being a volunteer for the ATP, George was a very successful businessman in a variety of endeavors. I asked him which of his businesses he was the most proud of.

George replied, and without a second's hesitation: "Oh, none of them. I am most proud of the three kids I raised! They are all winners and wonderful citizens. That makes me happy each and every day."

His response, and the pride in his voice as well as on his face, literally brought tears to my eyes. It was a very profound moment for me and is what *Raising Your Child to be a Champion in Athletics, Arts, and Academics* is all about: raising our children to be winners and wonderful citizens. If you do it right, as George Soper knew, it will make you happy each day and give you a friend for the rest of your life.

Wayne Shares His Formula with Me

*M*y relationship with Wayne Bryan began way back in 1972 as one of his very first tennis students in his clinics at the Cabrillo Racquet Club in Camarillo, California.

As with many coaches and pupils, we fell out of contact after I went to college and then moved further away to begin my own adult life, begin my own career and begin my own family.

Fortunately, shortly after the birth of my first child, Dallas Nicole, in 1987, Wayne and I reconnected. This was fortunate because Wayne shared with me his philosophies about his Formula and I was able to put them to use with both Dallas and Greg, who was born two years later.

Believe me, Wayne's Formula works! And not just in tennis.

Dallas could read before kindergarten and when she was in the first grade won a small contest and had her short winning essay printed in the local newspaper.

Wayne said if I did my job as a parent correctly, Dallas would one day be a great American novelist. "A female

Mark Twain," he said, with her books on the *New York Times* Best Seller List.

Silly, right? No sillier, Wayne pointed out, than parents doing all they can to help their child try to reach their dream of winning Wimbledon.

By using Wayne's blueprint, writing soon became Dallas's "Crazy Passion." When she was in the fifth grade, she won a grant to write and self-published her own book of short stories and poems. Her initial goal was to sell twenty-five copies and create her own $50 grant foundation. Instead, she sold more than 700 books and created two grants in her name! She was featured in the *Los Angeles Times* and *Girls' Life* magazine. She was asked to speak at local schools. The Santa Barbara Book Fair held a "Dallas Woodburn Day." Pretty heady stuff for anyone, let alone an eleven year old.

But Wayne saw it as just the beginning. He feels that success leads to more success when you help a child discover his or her "Crazy Passion." That has been true with Dallas, who has gone on to win state essay and national essay contests, been on the radio and TV numerous times, started her own Web site (www.zest.net/writeon) aimed at encouraging other youths to read and write, been featured in *CosmoGIRL* magazine as its Girl of the Month, and featured in the nationally-released book *So, You Wanna Be a Writer?*

Dallas wants to be on the *New York Times* Best Seller List when she grows up. And part of the reason is Wayne. After Dallas self-published her first book, Wayne bought a copy and gave her a check for $100. Dallas said that was too much, but Wayne told her it was a bargain for him because he was pre-paying to get a copy of every book she would write in the future. Talk about motivating a child and showing that you have confidence in her.

Another time, Dallas was doing a book signing for *So, You Wanna Be a Writer?* I was out of town so I couldn't be there. Well, Wayne shows up, pulls out his cell phone, calls me and starts going on and on about how poised Dallas's talk was and how terrific she is doing—all purposely within earshot of Dallas. Again, that made Dallas feel like a champion.

It is those kinds of sneaky "side-door" motivational things that will help you raise your child to be successful in writing or tennis or music or running (my son Greg's "Crazy Passion" is running and thanks to Wayne's Formula he is a national-class youth track and cross-country runner) or art or even bed making.

Yes, bed making. Wayne will tell you that his Formula can make your child into a champion bed maker if that is what you want. He's making a point, of course, but he's not far from the truth. I say this because looking back to my days in his youth tennis clinics, Wayne used "side-door" motivation to make us world champions at picking up trash. He did this by making cleaning up litter around the Cabrillo Racquet Club a game. While Wayne was saving money on janitor fees, we kids were having Fun!

Indeed, as you will see, Fun—with a capital F—is another major component of his Formula. If you follow Wayne's advice, your child will have Fun along his or her journey to excellence—and so will you.

All right, let's get started. Welcome to Wayne's world!

Raising Your Child to Be a Champion

in Athletics, Arts, and Academics

CHAPTER 1

Why Should You Raise a Champion?

*Success is peace of mind which is a direct result
of self-satisfaction in knowing you did your best to
become the best you are capable of becoming.*

—John Wooden

*W*hy should you raise a champion? Good question.
The answer is, quite simply, because everyone needs to
be a champion at something. This does not mean everyone
must try to be a tennis champion. Or a basketball champion. Or a fill-in-the-blank sports champion. How about a
champion musician? Or a champion student.

I believe a problem of perception comes from the term
"champion" or "winner." These words connote Little League
Dads and Stage Moms pushing their children to fulfill the
parents' own dreams rather than their child's dream. I am
strongly against pushing children. Rather, I feel you must
guide and direct. Only in this way are you able to help
your child realize his or her true potential. And that, really,

is what being a champion is: realizing your potential. As John Wooden says, "Being the best you are capable of becoming."

Indeed, my Formula is not an attempt to give a step-by-step blueprint for raising a Wimbledon champion or Super Bowl quarterback or World Series MVP or the next Mia Hamm. The goal should be to raise a champion under a broader definition. Perhaps being a champion means for a struggling student to eventually get straight B's on a report card. Or for a child with a physical challenge, such as an amputated leg, to ski down a hill. Or a kid to discover music, take lessons, start a band and win a school talent show—like my nephew, Josh, recently did in the span of a few months. There are endless definitions of a champion.

Being a champion means being fulfilled. Peace of mind and self satisfaction, remember. Unfortunately, society continues to take away opportunities for our children to feel fulfilled and to experience self-satisfaction. We make it harder to feel like champions. Too many schools have cut their music programs, cut their physical education classes and cut out the arts. In doing so, they take away the very things that make kids want to go to school. They take away some of their dreams.

You, then, must give your child something to be excited about, to dream about, to aspire to. Give them something he or she can try to become a champion at. That's just the first step, however. First the dream, then the accomplishment. Next, you have to give them the means for chasing, and hopefully reaching, their goals.

And here is the really cool thing, the exciting part for you as a parent: The very tools you give your child to use in striving to become a sports or music or academic champion are the very same life lessons he or she will need to survive—and thrive—in any endeavor. These tools include goal setting, daily scheduling, knowing and planning the steps to reach your dreams, and overcoming tough times.

In addition, your child, in striving to excel, will acquire the important character traits of dedication, perseverance, problem solving, and self-confidence.

Furthermore, when a child is focused on becoming a champion, focused on striving for excellence and trying to become the best he or she is capable of being, they will not have the inclination or time to take a negative path. They don't have to say "No" to drugs because they are so involved in their Passion that these destructive forces will have no place in their lives.

While striving to reach their goals, they will find themselves coming in contact with other young people who are also heading onward and upward. American tennis star and Olympic gold medallist, Lindsey Davenport, often speaks of how inspired she was by being around the other athletes competing in the 1996 Atlanta Games.

Even in the inner-cities, gangs are known to watch out for and protect young athletes (and even singers, violinists, artists, etc.) who display the talent to one day make it out of the poverty. Instead of recruiting these successful kids to join their gang, many gang members actually respect them and leave them alone.

The key is, you want your child focusing his/her energies on self-improvement, not self-destruction. As my young author friend, Dallas Woodburn, says, "Reach for the stars and you might grab a piece of the moon." I like that saying and attitude. That is what future champions do. They aim high for the stars and sometimes they reach that lofty goal. If not, they still stand a good chance of accomplishing something very worthwhile.

People often ask me if they should allow their child to dream of being a Wimbledon champion. After all, thousands and thousands of young tennis players throughout the world have this grand aspiration, and there are very few Wimbledon champs. I say, yes, shoot for the stars and chase your dreams. Even if you fall short it will be a journey with nice stops along the way while learning the great lessons of life.

CHAPTER 2

When Do You Start to Raise a Champion?

The ideal day never comes. Today is ideal for him who makes it so.

—Horatio Dresser

*W*hen should you start to raise a champion?

Now!

Immediately!

Don't wait even until tomorrow. Today is the ideal day to start. It's never too soon to start raising a champion. No skill is too difficult that it cannot be broken down into a beginning step that is so very simple that even the youngest child can have Fun mastering it.

Maybe the step or goal or challenge is as simple as touching a bouncing tennis ball with a racket. I actually blew up balloons for our 2-year-old twins to hit with toy tennis rackets to start helping their hand-eye coordination. They had lots of laughs and Fun chasing and whacking those balloons.

Maybe the goal is to strike a bass drum twice in a row. Heck, maybe it is as simple as having the young child just sit on the drum-set stool. I am not kidding. When I taught Mike and Bob the drums that is how we started. I made sitting on the stool without falling off the very first step, made it Fun, and congratulated them when they succeeded. And then we went from there.

The next step was to place their foot on the pedal. Then to stomp down on it hard enough to beat the drum. Then to do it twice in a row.

"Great, Mikey! Now can you do it four times in a row?" And so on.

Each step by itself seems silly in its simplicity, but remember that the great cathedrals were built one stone at a time. And also remember that each step, no matter how simple, must be accompanied with generous praise and encouragement.

Great rodeo stars always say, "I grew up on a horse." The Osmond Family siblings grew up singing and dancing in the living room at a very early age. If you read the ATP media guide, you will see that most of the pro tennis players were hitting balls by age 6. Youngsters in Japan are virtuosos on the violin before they even start school.

If a discipline is presented incrementally and in a Fun and stimulating way, kids are capable of amazing things. They are taking the first steps down the road to becoming a champion.

CHAPTER 3

Cornerstone of Wayne's Formula: Make It *Fun*!

Girls just wanna have fun!
—Cyndi Lauper

Cyndi Lauper is right, "Girls Just Wanna Have Fun!" But I have also found that boys just wanna have FUN, too. And babies just wanna have Fun. Moms and dads, grandmas and grandpas just wanna have Fun. We all just wanna have Fun. *Fun* with a capital *F*.

Fun. That's the whole ballgame as I see it. Indeed, Fun has to permeate all elements of the Formula. To raise a champion, you need to hook your child with Fun.

I'm a big believer that kids have Fun doing "ing" things. Here's what I mean by "ing" things: Smiling. Laughing. Playing. Dancing. Running. Jumping. Diving. Hitting a ball.

When you see "ing" you know a kid is having Fun. Kids having Fun can't wait to do it. They spend lots of hours doing it. Time flies by when they are doing it.

A survey of 10,000 high school athletes by the American Youth and Sports Participation study revealed that the No. 1 reason kids participate in sports is to have—you guessed it—Fun!

And the pivotal reason why kids drop out of sports? You guessed it again—it was not Fun!

But the importance of Fun goes beyond that. Dr. Ellen Langer, a professor of psychology at Harvard, has found that people learn best when they are at play. In other words, when they are having Fun. They learn faster, retain more and are more productive.

That is why field trips are so valuable. Kids having Fun at the Monterey Aquarium will learn more about marine biology than they could learn in 50 classroom hours.

It is the same in athletics. If you make it Fun to hit a

tennis ball, maybe by putting up a target of cans to knock down or offering chocolate chip cookies as a prize for hitting 100 shots over the net in a row, the child will learn faster.

The reverse is also true, Dr. Langer suggests. Those who aren't having Fun struggle to learn. So if you have a kid hit a thousand backhands off a ball machine while he is bored out of his mind, he's not going to learn very much. Except, probably, that tennis is boring!

Therefore, Fun must permeate everything for the Formula to work its magic. Taking the kids to watch a great USC vs. UCLA tennis match is a good way to have Fun. But it's not enough just watching the match. The kids have to have Fun in the car going there. Even if it drives you crazy, let the kids choose the music on the radio, for instance. They also have to have Fun getting pizza afterwards. Pizza to me says Fun. A van filled with kids says Fun. Even the anticipation of the trip itself must be Fun. And thinking back on the entire experience afterwards should be Fun.

Even pro superstars "wanna have Fun!" After his first game back in the NBA after coming out of retirement, Los Angeles Lakers superstar Magic Johnson said, "It was great. It was so much fun."

Conversely, I think about the Chicago Cubs superstar second baseman Ryne Sandberg who, despite still being a great player, walked away from baseball a few years ago with millions of dollars remaining on his contract. Asked why he was retiring, Sandberg replied: "I just wasn't having fun with baseball anymore."

He didn't want more money, he wanted more Fun.

If you think having Fun and being a champion are mutually exclusive, you couldn't be more wrong. Consider legendary basketball coach John Wooden, who led his UCLA teams to 10 NCAA national championships in a twelve-year span with seven of those titles coming consecutively.

"I looked forward to practice every day because it was the best part of my day," recalls Bill Walton, a member of two of those Bruin championship teams and now a member of the Basketball Hall of Fame. "Coach Wooden made practice a celebration of life. He made it so much fun. Sure, we were focused and we worked hard, but it was still always—always—fun."

And this is what U.S. Olympic figure skater Tara Lipinski said before she won the gold medal at the 1998 Winter Games: "If I don't get an Olympic medal, what am I left with? I want my Olympic memories. This is my chance to have fun."

I love that attitude. And I truly believe it was that attitude that helped her win the gold medal.

Rich Gallien, the women's tennis coach at USC, knows the value of having Fun while pursuing excellence. He wrote a letter to Mike and Bob dated April 14, 1994—I know the date because the boys still have his letter. Its message was so important: "Just remember one thing, have fun each day."

Have Fun each day! What a great motto to live your life by. French painter Camille Pissarro knew this. Famed as the "Father of Impressionism," he also made an impression on his offspring. Pissarro taught his children to paint, and they taught their children—in all, thirteen descendants became artists.

"He taught his children how to enjoy painting, how to see the fun in being able to draw," said Lelia Pissarro, one of his great-granddaughters. "It did not matter if it was good or bad, the point was to learn and enjoy, and that's something I've kept all my life."

The best coaches and teachers and mentors—and parents!—know how to make it enjoyable for their pupils or child. They make it Fun. Lots of coaches can have a tremendous amount of technical knowledge, but they can't impart it in a Fun way. I'll take the Fun coach over the technically superior coach, especially in the early going.

Indeed, you as a parent must find coaches and mentors who have the imagination and flexibility to take a unique approach and make the discipline—be it sports or music or whatever—Fun. It can't be drudgery. It has to be Fun. Without Fun, the Crazy Passion will not develop. And without Crazy Passion, there can be no champion.

Yes, it's important that a young basketball player learn the fundamentals of dribbling and pivoting and passing. But I say the coach should find a way to make them *Fun*damentals, because, believe me, you can get worse at something—basketball, tennis, music, painting—if it's stiff, monotonous and not Fun.

A perfect example of this is a book signing that my young friend Dallas Woodburn had last summer. I saw the announcement in the newspaper and when I showed up I was struck by the Fun atmosphere. There was 14-year-old Dallas, not standing behind a podium, but sitting on a table and surrounded by people of all ages. And next to her was a huge bowl of popcorn. Popcorn, like pizza, to me says Fun. And there was Fun music playing on the boombox. The organizers had obviously made an effort to create a Fun atmosphere. It worked. Instead of a speaking engagement, they had created a party.

Now let's change that scenario around. Let's take the popcorn and music away. Let's take the Fun out and make it an academic environment with stiff adults. That would have chilled Dallas out. That would have made her not want to strive to have future book signings. Instead of adding to her love for writing, it would have chipped away at her Crazy Passion for it. But by making it Fun, it becomes another positive stepping stone on her journey to becoming a champion author.

Coaches, teachers and parents often ask me: "How do you know it's Fun for the kid or kids I'm working with?" For me the litmus test is as easy as this: Is it Fun for the coach or teacher?

In the wonderful movie, *Mr. Holland's Opus,* the music teacher, played by Richard Dreyfuss, was frustrated and impatient with how slowly his students were learning the fundamentals. It all changed when he went with the Fun. Soon you see Mr. Holland smiling and leading his marching band down the street moving and grooving while they played the rock hit, "Louie, Louie."

Remember that Fun is contagious and Fun is the key to the kingdom. As Dr. Norman Vincent Peale said, "If there's no fun in it, something is wrong with all you're doing."

CHAPTER 4

Pushing the Passion Button with Side-Door Motivation

We may affirm absolutely that nothing great in the world has been accomplished without passion.

—George Wilhelm Friedrich Hegel

*M*ichelangelo did not paint the ceiling of the Sistine Chapel because someone told him to. He did so because it was his Passion. It is what he had to do. The result, as is so often the case when Passion is involved, was a true masterpiece.

Music, of course, was Elvis's Passion. Experimenting was Thomas Edison's Passion. Flying was the Wright Brothers' Passion—and Michael Jordan's Passion, too. No one told young Michael to spend all day, every day, on the playground shooting baskets. He wanted to. It was in his heart. He had to.

Your job as a parent is to help your child find his/her Passion. Your mission is also to make certain that his/her Passion is a positive one. You must play a role in helping your child find his or her Passion. Otherwise, Madison Avenue, your child's peers, TV, video games, or the street will all end up shaping and guiding your youngster's destiny for you.

Does that sound controlling? A Svengali-like attitude? If done in the typical way where a parent pushes and forces a child to do something, then yes, it is. For example, consider Marv Marinovich, who from the time his son Todd was an infant in a crib was programming him to be a football quarterback. The result was that Todd grew up to be a star quarterback in high school and at USC, and was even an NFL first-round draft pick by the Raiders. But then the moonshot exploded. Todd quit after two NFL seasons because it was not his dream. It was not his Passion. He was simply being forced to follow his father's dream. Ultimately, the result was a nightmare that included drugs and jail.

Such stories of burned out young athletes are far too common. You probably know a friend or neighbor whose son or daughter quit their sport in high school. The mistake so many parents make is they open the front door and try to push their child through it every day. They demand, "Go practice." "Go work out." "Go do it!"

This approach simply does not work. Nagging never does. It is far more effective to motivate your child through the side door.

Think of sports—or music, writing, art or school—like making a bed. Telling Jason or Jessica, "Go make your bed!" doesn't get very good results. Maybe for a week or two it works. But not in the long run.

If there were an ad campaign showing Derek Jeter or Beyoncé making beautiful hospital corners on their beds every morning, perhaps you'd have a chance. But there isn't such a TV ad. Or, if all your child's friends were fanatics about making their beds . . . but again, that isn't reality.

Reality is that telling Jason and Jessica, "Get in there and practice the Piano!" doesn't work any more effectively than demanding, "Jessica, go practice your tennis!" or "Jason, please get in there and study!"

Again, that might work in the short term. Maybe Jason will go into his room and open his math book. Or, more likely, he will turn on his stereo instead. Or fire up a video game. Maybe Jessica will go practice her backhand. Or maybe not. In truth, probably not.

They might shuck and jive and go through the motions as a coping mechanism. Make you think they are doing it. But they won't put their heart and soul into it. No one enthusiastically does what they are forced to do.

The key, then, is to push their Passion Button with Side-Door Motivation.

Here's my way of Side-Door Motivating in a Fun way. On Tuesday, I tell the kids at a tennis clinic, "On Friday bring $5 because I'll have a bus here at the club. Bring a sweatshirt because it will get a little chilly at night. We're going to see the USC Trojans play the UCLA Bruins. It's going to be an awesome match and anyone getting straight B's or better can go!" You should see the faces light up! The kids get excited. So do I, because to me a motivational event, like seeing a college match, is worth about thirty hours of practice in your discipline of choice be it sports, dance, music, art, writing, whatever.

That's right, it's worth thirty hours of practice. People laugh when I say this, but I am serious.

If you want to Side-Door Motivate your son to be a football player, take him to see the Rose Bowl game. Take him to see Stanford-Cal. Or if you want to motivate them to play baseball, take them to see Sammy Sosa and the Cubs play.

To Side-Door Motivate your daughter to be a singer, go to a Sheryl Crow or Vanessa Carlton concert. I see thousands of girls galvanized by them. If you want her to go into ice skating, go see Sarah Hughes or Michelle Kwan. If you want her to play basketball, go to college or WNBA games.

That's how you hook them—with Fun and Side-Door Motivation!

I not only took Mike and Bob to see Andre Agassi play, but at the matches we bought posters of Andre. Don't underestimate the value of that as Motivation. They covered their bedroom walls with posters of Andre. They saw those posters every day and it was a great way to keep them Motivated.

We also had subscriptions to tennis magazines come to the house. We even invited the twins' kindergarten class out to the tennis club for a clinic. I needed a couple of kids for a demonstration, and of course, chose Mike and Bob. Suddenly, they not only saw themselves as tennis players, their peers did also. In no time, Mike and Bob were wearing their wrist bands to school. Then they were wearing their tennis clothes to school. Then dragging their rackets to school. Look, I never said, "Hey, Mike and Bob, you should be tennis players." Instead, I took them to watch exciting tennis events.

I must point out, however, that Motivation changes as you move forward on your journey with your child. What Motivates a 4-year-old will not necessarily Motivate a 10-year-old and what Motivates a kid at 10 won't Motivate a 16-year-old. A parent or a coach needs to recognize these changes and appropriately adjust with new forms of Motivation. You must be creative, seeking new ways to keep your child passionate. Motivation must be continually fed.

Mike and Bob attended their first Davis Cup match when they were 10 years old. It was held at La Costa and the U.S. was playing Mexico. Before the doubles, I took the boys out to get some popcorn and as we were coming back down the tunnel to the courts who was walking up but American star, Ricky Leach, with his partner, Jim Pugh, on their way to enter the stadium.

Ricky said, "Hi, Twins."

With their eyes wide as saucers the brothers said in unison, "Hi Ricky!"

"Been playing any tournaments?" Ricky asked.

"Yeah. We just won Long Beach last Sunday," said Mikey.

"Good job, guys. I won that tournament too."

Ricky and Jim went out and won their match in four exciting sets and Mike and Bob were pumped and waving miniature U.S. flags the whole time from the front row. Mike and Bob returned home more hooked on tennis than ever and thinking that since they won the same junior tournament Ricky Leach once won, they could someday make the big time too.

However, you don't have to Motivate your child with quintessential events. You don't have to take your child to grand events such as the Davis Cup, Wimbledon, or the U.S. Open. It's just as exciting for a young child to go see USC vs. UCLA.

Go to a great high school tennis match. Indeed, I strongly believe in attending high school events for grade school kids. To a grade school kid a high school athlete is a god. And the event itself is Motivational. The next step of progression is to see college athletes perform. And then professionals.

In music, you do not have to go see U2 or Bruce Springsteen. Go see a small touring band. Or a local high school band. Go see a garage band next door. In fact, go to all of these because it highlights the road of progression. For me, it was not enough to Motivate Mike and Bob by exposing them to top-flight tennis.

Similarly, if we are talking about music, it is not only about exposing a child to Carnegie Hall. Sure, that is great and important. But it is also important to take them to a local concert. Take them to a high school show. Play classical CDs in the car stereo and at home. It all sinks in, the little stuff as well as the grand.

In my case, I took Mike and Bob to see professional tennis matches at the Mercedes Benz Cup in Los Angeles. But I also took them to see college players and even good high school matches. Heck, when they were 6, I'd show them good 10-year-olds playing. To a 6-year-old, a kid four years older can seem like a world champion.

This was vital because that was the next progression for them, to be as good as a 10-year-old.

And then you go from there. Take them to a high school match (or concert) and then a college match (or production) and then a pro match (or Broadway play).

By showing them every level, they see the progression it takes to get to where they ultimately want to go. By seeing a high school player, they will not be as intimidated by a pro and think, "I could never be that good." They shoot for becoming a top high school player first.

When Davis Cupper Ricky Leach told Mike and Bob that he had won the same junior tournament as they had, the twins saw the progression: Gee, if you win such-and-such tournament you might one day be good enough to play Davis Cup.

Now, maybe you can't introduce your child to Ricky Leach or Cheryl Miller, but you certainly can introduce him/her to a college player. On the other hand, take them to a clinic and maybe they can meet Pete Sampras or Michael Jordan after all.

CHAPTER 5

Less Is More

Happiness is a way station between too little and too much.

—Channing Pollock

With Side-Door Motivation, instead of pushing your child through the front door, just open a side door a crack.

Let me share an example. A lot of people have read that Hall of Fame basketball star Pete Maravich, when he was young, would dribble his basketball while riding his bike to the movies and then would actually dribble it in the aisle during the show. He would also shoot baskets until it was too dark outside to even see the rim and backboard. But what you may not know is how Pete's Passion started.

It started when his father, Press, would wait outside for his son to come home from grade school. As soon as he saw Pete approaching, Press would start shooting baskets and then quit right when young Pete came up the driveway.

Pete, of course, would beg his father to shoot some with him, but Press would say he was already tired from shooting and then go inside. Soon, Pete was racing home to get there before his dad got tired and quit. At the same time, Press started staying out just a little longer.

The father's Passion became the son's Passion, too. Pete was eventually named one of the NBA's All-Time 50 Greatest Players.

Earl Woods, the father of the golfing great, Tiger Woods, said in his book, Raising a Tiger, he wanted to always keep his son "wanting more" on the golf course. When Tiger was little he saw how much his dad enjoyed playing golf

and asked if he could practice with him. After a very long pause, his father would say, "All right," but he would always make sure that his young son didn't hit too many balls at one time.

Mike and Bob would watch me give tennis lessons at the club when they were 2 years old. Afterwards, they would always ask me to hit a couple balls to them and I would say, "Okay, but just a couple." The forbidden fruit just made them want to do it more.

I fed just a couple of balls to each of them. They begged for more but I would stop. The next day, I'd let them hit for a little longer, and then again quit while they still wanted more. You get the picture.

In fact, even as Mike and Bob became nationally ranked junior players, Kathy, and I would make them stop practicing before they wanted to call it a day. People have a hard time believing this, but we never once asked Mike and Bob to practice—but boy have we had to fight with them to get them off the courts!

Here is a story that illustrates Side-Door Motivation and at the same time, how setting limits can keep the child wanting more.

I took Mike and Bob, when they were 5 years old, to see The Ojai Tennis Championships, the largest and longest running amateur tournament in the United States. The Center Court is in a majestic park with huge oak and sycamore trees. When the stands are packed it is an incredibly inspiring setting. When Mike and Bob first gazed upon the scene, they were breathless for what seemed like five minutes. Their eyes got big and you could almost hear their little minds thinking, "Wow. I want to play here someday."

It only lasted a short time, however, and the next thing I knew, the boys had raced off to the nearby creek in the park to catch frogs. But that didn't matter. The effect had taken place. The seed had been planted. Now it only needed watering and care.

The point is, I didn't force them to leave the frogs alone and come sit with me through a two-hour match. That would have undone the magic that had just taken place. I had accomplished my goal: the twins were exposed to something wonderful and it had made an impression on them.

The following year when we came back to The Ojai, Mike and Bob did not want to chase the frogs, they wanted to watch some of the great tennis—for a short while anyway. And the third year back, they sat and watched even longer.

And that is how a Passion grows. Like a fire, it is lighted and then you fan the flames, ever so gently mind you, until it bursts into a roaring blaze. But be careful. If you fan the early sparks too vigorously, you will extinguish them.

The less-is-more approach is a key element in the Formula. The natural eagerness and enthusiasm of a child should be carefully and thoughtfully managed so there is lots left over for another day.

CHAPTER 6

The Two P's: Praise and Positive Reinforcement

He took the praise as a greedy boy takes apple pie.

—Lord Macaulay

*I*n my experience as a teaching pro, I have found that as a motivator, praise and positive reinforcement work far better than pain or punishment. In fact, pain and punishment, like nagging and pushing, don't work at all in the long run. When you praise, shout it to the rooftops and if you must criticize, drop it like a dandelion. On second thought, don't criticize at all.

The best coaches and mentors and teachers are the ones who know the power of "the pat on the back." Sports and academics and the performing arts can knock you flat on your back sometimes. The great coach, teacher or parent understands the difficulty in any performing endeavor and the vulnerability of the player or singer or actor or writer. They are quick to lend a helping hand to pull them back

up on their feet, dust them off so they can venture out onto the stage or court once again.

Here is a story that illustrates that it is often the nice and well-meaning parent who is inadvertently destructive to the child's self-esteem and confidence. However, I will change the names to protect the guilty.

Kathy and I have a dear and long-time friend named Larry Kruel. We had Larry over to the house for a BBQ. His lovely daughter, Janie, was in our music room singing while Bob and Mike accompanied her on the drums and piano. I called out to Larry, who was in the middle of a croquet game, "Come in here and listen to Janie sing!"

His daughter had been working hard for over a year on her vocals and had performed a few times with our band at various gigs. She was much improved and has a very nice voice. She and the guys did a super rendition of the U2 hit song, "Beautiful Day." When they finished, Kathy and I clapped enthusiastically. Larry, however, with an attempt at humor, remarked, "Don't quit your day job." Needless to say, we all ripped Larry unmercifully for his thoughtless remark.

Be careful with those hurtful remarks when your child is performing and putting it on the line.

"Gee. What happened out there today, Joey? . . . You beat him last time . . . Why am I wasting money on those lessons?" These kind of comments can flatten a child's self-esteem and take the Fun out of their endeavor.

I've seen a mom sit and watch a two-hour tennis match with a yellow legal pad in hand. She took notes on each and every point that was played. And after the match, she sat her 14-year-old daughter down and reviewed her child's performance with statements like: "Betty, at 4–3 in the third set, you had a backhand passing shot and you hit it down the line. You should have hit it crosscourt."

Betty, after losing the tough match 6–4 in the third set, is already sitting on the bench figuratively bleeding and wounded. The last thing she wants to do is rehash every mistake she made. On most shots she had less than a second to react and was doing the best she could out there.

Look, I know that some days nothing goes right up on that stage or on that court. On those days when Joey strikes out four times in a row, Billy loses 6–0, 6–0 or Susie is singing flat, that's when you've really got to come up with something positive.

"Your uniform looked so good on you today," or "I loved your sportsmanship out there," or "What a super attitude you had," or "Your smile was just fantastic." Always find *something* positive to say.

Also frame all your coaching in a positive way. Don't use negative words. Don't say: "That's not how to swing." Instead say, "Boy, that swing is getting smoother and smoother." Don't use words that end in n't, like I just did in this paragraph.

You can encourage your child not only with praise and positive words, but also with little rewards that can be fun and hugely effective.

When Mike and Bob were very small, they would drag me to the tennis courts early every Saturday morning to see if they could hit 100 shots over the net without a miss. Why? Because if they did, they could go up to the snack bar and have a giant oatmeal raisin cookie. I could have threatened them with running laps or pushups or some other punishment and they might have hit 100 in a row. Or perhaps, more likely, they might have missed on purpose to defy the challenge. Hitting 100 shots in a row would have been a chore instead of a game. But by putting a cookie on the line, it became Fun and positive. I have said it many times, Mike and Bob Bryan are the champions built by cookies!

There are many other ways to reward a child. Kinder-garten teachers know that their young students perform better when they give them a sticker or a gold star for a job well done. Give your child a sticker for hitting five shots in a row. Give her a gold star for playing chopsticks on the piano. Reward a child both early and often. Delayed gratification means delayed success.

Let's say Johnny has learned how to play a new song on the piano. Okay, every time Grandma comes over, the first thing you do is have Johnny play Grandma his new song. He is thus rewarded for his success in learning a new song and also rewarded with Grandma's attention.

As adults we often forget how special trophies and trinkets and ribbons are to children. They are very special!

That is why you must display your child's trophies, even if they are just for participating in an event. Put the trophy on the fireplace mantle for a while and then move it into the child's room. As the trophies mount up, build a shelf of honor for them. Then add more shelves as needed. Trophies, medals and ribbons are a great reminder of successes and a big booster of confidence and Motivation all at once. So display them where the child and visitors can see them.

For example, in our home Mike and Bob's gold tennis ball awards for winning national titles were—and still are!—proudly displayed on the piano where they would be constant reminders at least one hour a day when they were playing music.

Frame certificates and awards, and hang them on the wall. Similarly, frame photos of your child playing or performing and display them. Again, this shows them that what they do is special and reinforces their identity as a tennis player or golfer or musician. And, obviously, if the discipline is art, frame and hang many of their paintings, and also give some pieces to relatives and friends as well for them to hang on their walls.

Another thing you can do is make scrapbooks to look at later and take videos of matches or games or recitals to watch later. Both of these are great ways to be reminded of past success and serve as great Motivation for future success.

Hang ribbons and newspaper clippings on the refrigerator, and frame longer stories to hang on the wall. Also, be sure to mail copies of stories to relatives to reinforce to the child how proud you are.

Hang good grade cards on the refrigerator, too. As you can tell, I love refrigerator doors because kids see what's posted here numerous times a day. These things all provide Motivation and a sense of accomplishment.

I remember when Kathy took Mike and Bob to their first tennis tournament at Lake Lindero when they were 6 years old. Darned if they didn't win it! I can't tell you how much those trophies meant to them. If you have a child who has gotten a team trophy in AYSO soccer or Little League baseball, you know what I mean. A trophy or ribbon can Motivate a child even more than Grandma's attention or a big cookie!

Growing up with success, no matter how small, is in itself great Motivation. People like awards and the roar of the crowd. Adulation can propel a child forward. Be it a gold star or sticker, ribbon or trophy, Grandma's kisses or a big cookie, rewards have many positive effects on the child. "Hey, I'm good at this . . . I'm a winner . . . I'm successful . . . If I practice, I'll get even better . . . Hey, this is *fun*!"

CHAPTER 7

The Steps of Progression

Knowledge advances by steps, and not by leaps.

—Lord Macaulay

*B*ecoming a champion in sports, or becoming a great musician or artist, is like building the pyramids one block at a time.

In tennis, an early step might be, "Can you roll this ball across the court with your racket? . . . Congratulations! . . . Okay, can you balance the ball on your strings without dropping it? . . . Great!"

"Now walk around while balancing it? . . . Now run? . . . Can you touch the ball with the racket when I feed it to you? . . . Can you hit it over the net from the service line? . . . One out of five times? . . . Five in a row? . . . Now one in five from the baseline? . . . Now on the dead run?"

In music, you start by asking, "Can you find Middle C?" Then you move on to a combination of two notes, then three, and so on.

"Can you hit the bass drum four times in a row? . . . Great!"

"Now can you do it in even time? . . . Super!"

"Next week I'll give you a new drum game."

That's right, I use the word "game" instead of "drill" or "task." Make it a game. Make it Fun. Use relays and balloon targets and turn tennis practice into recess with rackets. Remember, Fun must always permeate the Formula. We learn better when we are having Fun.

I say set up little steps that are impossible to fail at. The best teacher/coach/mentor has an ability to take any task, no matter how difficult, and break it down to the

bottom step. In teaching the drums to a small child, this means having Fun learning how to climb up on the stool! Like I said, set it up so the child can't fail!

For the past five years I have been conducting tennis clinics across the nation in stadiums during pro events and I've never yet had a kid come out of the stands and fail at hitting the tennis ball. The thing is, I don't start these kids at Step 37. I don't feed them the ball on the run at the baseline. Instead, I set it up so they can't fail. I stand them 8 feet from the net and give them a soft, perfect feed. If they miss the first ball, I give them a second and a third. Heck, if I need to, I will feed them 10 balls at once and when they swing there is no way they won't hit one of them over the net. In fact, sometimes they hit two or even three balls over with one swing!

The crowd, of course, cheers for the young player and I give him a prize. And meanwhile he thinks, "Hey, tennis is Fun." And all the youngsters in the crowd watching him are enjoying it as well. Then I say, "Isn't this easy?" instead of what most coaches say, which is, "Isn't this hard?"

You see, if you get them playing and having Fun first, then they can learn the proper mechanics later. It just makes sense to start out simple and then go from there. I mean, in kindergarten our first assignments are ones we can't fail at, right? In art, for instance, it is finger painting. How can you fail at that? You can't! The Mona Lisa-like masterpieces come later.

I can't emphasize this enough: The little steps are gigantically important. If you blow these first little steps, you don't let the child in. Instead of Side-Door Motivation, you will have dead-bolted the door closed!

Let me share a personal example. My brother, Carl, has skied his whole life and is a great skier. One day when we were both in college, he said, "Hey Wayne, let's go to the slopes and I'm gonna teach you how to ski."

"Okay, CB, I'm in."

When we arrived at the mountain my brother said, "Wayne, look, you're a great athlete. Let's just go on up to the top of the mountain and ski down."

"Okay, bro."

When we got to the top, I fell off the chair lift crashing into a couple of cursing skiers. When I got back on my feet CB said, "Okay. Here's how you do it."

He then gave me a five second demo and said, "Use your poles and get on those edges when you turn." And *swoosh*, he was off down the face of the mountain like Jean-Claude Killey.

How did I do? Well, I went straight down the face of the mountain at approximately 5 miles per hour and quickly sped up to what seemed like 100 mph. I was a blur. I became a human cannonball. When this great athlete finally fell, I fell for about a quarter of a mile. My skis were long gone, I had pulled half the muscles in my body and was lacerated and bleeding profusely.

But the worse thing of all was that every skier on the slope was laughing uncontrollably at me.

Needless to say, that is the last time I ever went skiing. When people now ask, "How about joining us on a ski trip up to Mammoth?" I say, "You gotta be outta your mind!"

You see, it wasn't Fun and my brother, now a well respected Superior Court Judge and community leader in

Nevada City, California, hadn't taught me the small steps. He'd been skiing for 10 years and it was easy for him. He wasn't able to break it down into the smallest steps for me. He should have, of course, taken me to a bunny slope and taught me step by step, beginning with putting my skis on and standing up.

Skill development must be sequential, but first and foremost it must be Fun. At the same time, after the very early stages, the new steps must also pose slight challenges. If it is too easy, for too long, the child will lose interest and will have no sense of accomplishment either. Too difficult, on the other hand, and the child will get frustrated and shut down. It's a fine line.

In other words, find the child's comfort zone, let her fully master a step in this zone and then stretch her just a little bit by moving on to the next step. Then the process repeats itself as the child must master a new skill before advancing further along the steps of progression.

It's funny. As parents, we get so excited when our child takes his first steps walking, but then we lose this enthusiasm along the way. I say we must show that same awe and wonderment when our child takes his first strum on the guitar or her first swing at the golf ball or her first glide on figure skates. Always continue showing that excitement and pride with each and every step of progression.

It takes thousands of steps to go from a 6-year-old learning how to hold a drum stick to playing drums in front of 10,000 people, or from a 2-year-old trying to hit a balloon in his living room to playing on the Centre Court Wimbledon.

CHAPTER 8

Going for the Goal

Ah, a man's reach should exceed his grasp,
Or what's a heaven for?

—Robert Browning

*I*t is not only a progression of programming skills that you must know and follow. You must also know and follow a progression of goals. It is like colored belts in Karate. You can't become a black belt until you have progressed through white, yellow, orange, purple and brown along the way.

In tennis, it is the same. Can you become No. 4 in your age group at your local tennis club? No. 1? Can you be No. 3 at your high school? No. 1? Can you be top-10 in your state? Top-10 in the national juniors? Can you get a full-ride scholarship to Stanford? Can you get ranked in the top-10 in the world in doubles? Can you play Davis Cup?

Can you find the Middle C? Can you play chopsticks? Can you play a rock'n'roll groove? Can you form a band and rehearse? Can you win a school talent show?

Can you play a piece by Mozart? Can you play it at your July 4th BBQ? Can you play Mozart in Carnegie Hall?

Can you write a short story? Can you get it published in the local newspaper? Can you write a short book? Can you be featured in a national magazine? Can you be featured in a nationally-published book? Can you make the *New York Times* Best Seller List? Can you win a Pulitzer Prize?

You get the idea. A progression of goals. Without setting goals, you are driving to a vacation spot you have dreamed about but without a road map to help get you there.

Shane Battier, the John Wooden Award-winner as college basketball's player of the year in 2001, is an example of how important goal-setting can be for Motivation and guidance. Ever since he was 10 years old, Battier, now an NBA star, has made up a list of 10 goals on an index card every New Year's Eve and then taped it to his bedroom wall where he would see the goals daily. At the end of the year he would cross off the goals attained and make a new list, often with any unaccomplished goals put back on it.

Like Battier, I am a big believer in goals. I especially believe these six things about goals:

1. Goals must be short term and long term.

I say you must have long-term goals, but really these are more like dreams. For an 8-year-old to say he wants to play Davis Cup doubles or a 12-year-old to say she wants to win a Pulitzer Prize is ridiculously unrealistic, and yet it is also important. When he was very young, Tiger Woods made out a list of Jack Nicklaus' professional golf records and made goals of topping them—and now look what Tiger is doing! Don't take dreams away from your child.

Short-term goals, meanwhile, help you reach long-term goals and should be broken down into weekly, monthly, and yearly goals. Anything beyond that tends to become a long-term dream.

2. Goals must be realistic.

In other words, the goal can't be unattainable. It is very frustrating to have a goal not met. You should have to stretch to reach it, yes, but not stretch to the breaking point.

3. Goals must be specific.

"I want to get better," is not a specific goal. "I want to get an A in English," is specific. "I want to improve my time in the mile to under 6 minutes." "I want to be able to play every chord on the guitar by Feb. 15."

I also like numerical goals whenever possible. In tennis, rankings goals—such as to be top-5 at my club or varsity at my high school team or No. 1 in my state—are excellent. You have to be specific to be terrific.

If the discipline is writing, a specific numerical goal might be, "I want to enter 10 contests this year." Even better, make it into two even more specific goals: "I want to enter five short-story contests" and "I want to enter five poetry contests."

It is important to have multiple goals—this gives the child more chances for small success along the way to great success. Especially with younger ages, the child can ask for your help setting up goals. If so, help them—make suggestions and ask questions—but let the child actually choose the goals.

Goals can, and should, be revised and tweaked from time to time. Perhaps the child is ahead of schedule so the challenges need to be upped. Or maybe the goals need to be slowed down due to injuries or just plain bad luck. However, do not cave in too soon. There is no greater satisfaction than overcoming adversity to achieve a goal.

4. Goals must be written down by the child.

I like the goals typed on a computer by the child. Writing a goal down imprints it on the child's brain. This triggers

Motivation in the child. Having a goal written down, or saved in a computer file, is also a very valuable tool to check back on at a later date. Perhaps during a time a child is struggling with a new set of goals, she can gain confidence by reviewing past goals she has already accomplished.

5. Goals should be posted on the bathroom mirror and on the refrigerator.

This constantly reminds the child where she wants to go and provides the constant Motivation needed to get there.

6. Goals should be proclaimed to parents, coaches, friends and relatives.

I really like for the child to circulate his goals widely. Send the list of goals to grandparents and friends and teachers and the mentor and coach. This is something that is unique to me, but I believe in it strongly—the child will get support from these people and he needs that support!

A couple of examples. "Ms. Clark, I need a 4.0 grade point average to get into the University of Michigan next fall and I'll really need an A in your English class. That's my goal and I'll do everything I can to get that grade. Can you think of extra things I can do to get that A? Can you help me with this goal?" What will Ms. Clark do? I bet she'll do everything she can to help you and guide you to getting that A.

"Hey Coach McCampbell, I really need to be top-10 in SoCal by June 15th so I can get into the National Championships at Kalamazoo this summer. What can we do to step it up? I'm playing more tournaments and practice matches each week, do you have other ideas for me? Can you help me?"

"Uncle Wayne, our band is entering the district talent show and we want to get in there and win the thing. Can you help us learn a song so we can win the $50 first prize?"

"Grandma Williams, I want to go to a music camp this summer to increase my chances of getting in the high school jazz band next fall. Can I help do yard work around your house in June and July to earn money to pay for my camp fee?"

Mike and Bob religiously wrote down their goals each year. And you know what? They eventually achieved every single one of them from the time they were 8 years old up until they were 20. And now as professional athletes, they are still writing down their goals and going after them.

CHAPTER 9

The Daily Schedule Is Worth Its Weight in Gold

Do not squander time, for that's the stuff life is made of.

—Benjamin Franklin

*H*aving a daily schedule is every bit as important as having a tennis racket if that is your sport, or having a piano if music is your endeavor, or having paint and brushes if you are pursuing excellence in art. Without a daily schedule, you simply will not come close to finding enough time in each day to accomplish your goals.

A lot of things in your child's daily schedule should be automatic. The more things that are automatic, the better off they are. For example, they sleep 8 hours, they eat three times a day, shower (hopefully!) once a day, and make their bed (hopefully!). Also add in an automatic seven hours of school, Monday through Friday.

Well, just like those things, I believe your child's Passion should also automatically have time set aside. In fact, I believe children should spend a set amount of time on their Passion each day.

I'm a fanatic about the daily schedule. Mind you, it is not set in cement and can vary from day to day, but it still must be planned.

For example, Mike and Bob would get up early each morning to finish their homework and play some music. They knew they had school from 8 a.m. until 3 p.m. The bus dropped them off at the club where they were in the tennis program with all the other kids from 3 to 6 p.m. That was a given. They didn't have to find time for their Passion because it was automatic.

Same with their homework. They knew they would do school assignments and reading from 7 to 9 p.m. every night after eating dinner and relaxing.

Now, if you inject hours of watching TV or playing video games daily into this mix, then something has to give. After all, you can't not go to school. You shouldn't skip meals. It's not healthy to cut down on sleep, either. That means in order to watch TV you have to pull those hours out of music or tennis or homework. And you don't want that to happen.

Without a daily schedule, I believe it is flat-out impossible to become a champion in the classroom and in your Passion.

What is the parent's role in facilitating this daily schedule? Here are some specific steps.

Provide a clean and quiet study area for your child. Make sure your child has a healthy breakfast each morning and dinner at night, right on time. Transportation to school and after school should always be reliable. Make sure your child is involved in a supervised program that enhances her Passion. No time should be spent in the home by themselves!

And note, kids should be with other kids. Even if they play piano or golf or tennis, which would seem to be solitary pursuits, it is especially important to be involved with other youngsters who share that Passion. It's more Fun and more Motivational. The easiest way to achieve this Fun environment is to get in an established program in your community. You can also invite children with similar interests to your home to play some music together or hit putts in the backyard or practice a new dance routine.

Go to tournaments or other events in vans with other children. Parents can really help each other and at the same time make it more Fun and Motivational by sharing rides. "You drive this week and I'll drive next week."

You also need to schedule meets, events, tournaments, recitals, and writing contests with your child. This schedule of events is very important and, along with the goals, must be posted on the refrigerator door to serve as constant Motivation. Your child should always be looking forward to and preparing for an upcoming event.

The soccer season. The Little League baseball schedule. The school band concerts. The theatre department's upcoming plays. The Junior Team Tennis league schedule. These are examples of getting your child into a program that will put structure into their Passion.

Children can't practice in the abstract. They have to always be getting ready for a performance, a game, or meet. And the better the daily schedule, the more they will be Motivated and the better they will perform. It's the consistency and quality of that daily schedule that will produce champions.

CHAPTER 10

Play First, Learn Later

Experience gives us the test first and the lessons later.

—Naomi Judd

A good coach or teacher will emphasize playing first and learning later.

If an 8-year-old joined our tennis club on Wednesday with his mom, I would say, "Hi Billy. Welcome aboard. How about joining our Junior Team Tennis 10 & Under Novice Team? We play Westlake next Monday and we'd really like you to play the doubles for us."

"But Mr. Bryan, I've never played before and don't even have a racket."

I'd give Billy a big smile and say, "That's okay, Billy. Don't worry, we always beat Westlake."

What did little Billy do? He borrowed a racket and took his mom out to the court to feed him balls. He hit balls on the backboard all weekend. The programming drove the practice. By Monday, Billy was excited and ready to go

join our 10 & Under squad members in their quest against Westlake.

Did Billy win that first match? Like I said, we always beat Westlake. I gave Billy a good partner and most importantly, he had Fun.

Too many music teachers have a young piano student play scales for endless hours before they let them play a song. And when they finally let them try a song, it's "Santa Lucia" or "Drink to Me Only with Thine Eyes," rather than the latest pop song on the radio that they are dying to learn and play.

What's the job of a coach or music teacher? To me, first and foremost, it's to help the child enjoy the game or the instrument. Like it. Love it. Become Passionate about it. That's the ballgame.

Here's the story of how my wife Kathy got started in tennis. She went with her family to a summer church camp called Camp Awongo in the San Bernardino Mountains. She was 10 and had never picked up a tennis racket in her life. Her mom entered her in the camp tennis doubles championships with an elderly retired military officer who was a pretty fair player. She was the youngest and he was the oldest player in the tournament.

To make a long story short, Kathy and her partner won the tournament and she got a nice trophy. When she got home she asked, "Mom, when's my next tennis tournament? I like this game."

Kathy's tennis journey was rolling out beautifully from her first time playing at Camp Awongo. But listen to what happened next . . .

When Kathy got home her mom enrolled her in lessons with a local pro. He was, however, adamant about Kathy having to take lessons for one year before she could go out and compete again. Luckily, Kathy's mom took her to another coach who encouraged her to keep playing tournaments while he helped her develop her skills.

Kathy went on to become the National 16 & Under Junior Girls champ and a successful touring pro. Her entrée to the sport was through playing the game. She learned as she went and as she became better and better, she then got the coaching to take her to higher levels.

Mike and Bob's musical journey also came close to being derailed early on.

Mike and Bob had played music from an early age because we made it Fun from the get-go. The instruments were always set up and ready to play. We had my band members always visiting and jamming. We went to see other bands perform and the boys would ride along with me to my gigs. Even as 6-year-olds, they would come out of the audience to play and the crowds would love them. They played for our family, friends, neighborhood kids, classmates, and their pals at the tennis club.

They loved everything about music.

Then one day I said to Kathy, "Hey, we teach the boys tennis, why don't we get someone else to work on their music?"

So we signed them up for weekly piano lessons for Bob and drum lessons for Mike. And keep in mind, at age 6 they were already playing songs and performing.

After a few months, the boys came to us and said, "We don't want to go to our lesson today. We don't want to play music anymore. We don't like it."

"What!?"

"We don't like it."

"Let's don't cancel at this late time. I'll go to your lesson with you today and you can quit next week."

"Okay."

I went with them and here's what I saw: Mike, who had been playing a full trap set of drums, now was in a tiny studio playing little quarter notes and eighth notes on a drum pad. There was no life in his face as he went through these boring routines. Bob's teacher in his studio was saying, "Come on, Bob, that's an A flat not an A!"

Whoops. There was no Fun in it. I had made the mistake of not finding the right teacher or coach, which I'll address in the next chapter.

"Okay, guys. You can stop the lessons."

It wasn't too long, though, before Mike and Bob were back in our music room jamming with their friends and having a blast with their music. They have become fine musicians and have played gigs all across the country. Out on the tennis tour, they travel with their keyboard and guitar, and play with fellow pros every night in their hotel room. It's their release and it's Fun.

They get the sheet music of the songs they hear on the radio and work them out, note for note. They love music and they love playing with friends and they love performing.

It does no good for kids to play scales and learn music theory until they are bored out of their minds and can't wait to quit. I say, play first, learn later. The greatest drummers I have ever played with never took lessons. Great guitar players just sit in their bedroom at night and jam for hours.

Lots of great dancing comes from the street. Most surfers in the world didn't take surfing lessons. Remember, the best basketball players didn't have coaches when they first started playing. How do youngsters learn how to play basketball? They play basketball at the park all day. They play games like "H-O-R-S-E," "Around the World," and "Tip-In." They play one-on-one, two-on-two, three-on-three. They play half-court and full-court. They have free-throw shooting contests. They have three-point shooting contests.

Their skills develop out there on the playground through games and competition. If they lose, they sit down and if they win they stay in.

Look at what kids are doing on skateboards and snowboards these days. Amazing, isn't it? No one got in the way of their creativity and they were allowed to push the envelope. They played first and learned as they went. So many kids are lost early because teachers and coaches make music or tennis or golf boring. How can drums not be a blast for a child if we let them roll a little bit and gradually learn the nuances and fundamentals?

The coach and teacher must understand these basic principles of learning. A child or adult at play learns so much faster and retains so much more. Make it Fun and the rest will follow.

CHAPTER 11

Finding the Right Coach

To create within the athletes an interest and
enthusiasm for the events . . . then direct that
interest and enthusiasm along the lines of sound
fundamentals, taught imaginatively, purposefully
and even inspirationally.

—Brutus Hamilton

Finding the right coach, music teacher or mentor for your child is of paramount importance. Too many parents just take their child to a coach or teacher who is conveniently located. They haven't checked him out.

If you were going to buy a car or a house you would surely spend some time checking around. Do the same when searching for someone to help your child along their road to their dreams. You must phone around and ask others to help you find the coach or instructor who makes it Fun and who can Motivate and inspire.

Here's the kind of questions you should ask: Which coach or program has the most kids in it? Where's the action? Who has the most champions? Who is likable? Who has the charisma?

Then go meet this coach. See if he seems to have Fun

while teaching and working with the youngsters in his charge. Remember, I have yet to see a student not have Fun when the teacher was having Fun.

Ask the coach what he does to make a child have Fun while learning. Let your child take a couple of lessons and see if your child does indeed have Fun. If not, keep looking.

Finally, does the coach know the path to the top and all the stops along the way. Does he get his students playing and performing and competing right away? Does he set your child up with other children, whether it be playing tennis or golf or playing music or dancing? Kids love to be out there with other youngsters.

And the litmus test comes after the first lesson or clinic. Ask your child if she wants to go back again.

"Did you like the coach and did you have fun yesterday?"

"Yeah, Mom, I sure did. Can we go over there every day?"

That's the right teacher or coach for your child.

Don't focus too much at first on finding a coach who is technically excellent. The higher a child climbs on the skill ladder, the more important the technical aspects will become, but early on it is vital to find a coach who makes things Fun for your child. Obviously, you do not want a coach who has no technical knowledge, but he must more importantly have a positive personality and teaching method that connects with kids in a Fun way. I cannot emphasize enough that Fun must permeate everything.

If your child progresses beyond the technical skills of a certain coach, don't worry. A good coach will help you find a new coach to continue the journey with your child. And be sure to thank and appreciate that first coach because no matter what happens down the road, the most important coach of all is the one who made things Fun and helped start and stoke the fire of your child's Passion.

CHAPTER 12

Instill Values in Your Champion

*The simple word "Thanks" is one of the most
underused words in our language.*

—John Wooden

*Y*our child must not be allowed to be so focused
on his Passion that he forgets human values.
For me, this begins with thanking and appreci-
ating those who help your youngster along the road. This
includes thanking those who run a tournament or those
who put on a track meet or music recital, or the person
who stages a writing contest.

Your child must always say "thank you." No exceptions.

Your child must always write a thank-you note. Again,
no exceptions.

It's this simple: Losers look for thanks, praise and congratulations. Winners give thanks, praise and congratulations.

Woody Woodburn, who has written about some of the biggest names in sports, echoes this by pointing out that those who have sent thank-you notes for columns he has written on them include the likes of Jim Murray, John Wooden, Pat Riley, Greg Norman and Anthony Munoz. All of them are champions in the truest sense of the word.

I like the act of writing a thank-you note because it instills in a child a sense of appreciation. After all, without a tournament director, there would be no tournament to play in. So write and thank the director for his efforts. Mike and Bob always did this and still do. When they were young, I would of course help them address the envelope, but as they got older it was something they did on their own without any prodding. In fact, they even wrote thank-you notes to tournament volunteers who helped them and to writers who did stories on them.

I can't emphasize thank-you notes enough. Without someone putting in the time and effort to organize and hold a track meet, there would not be opportunities to compete. And without track meets, there is no serious running. I mean, I don't think a child would run with true Passion and effort if there were not others to compete against. Sure, he might run, but it wouldn't be the same.

This goes for any organized event. Someone puts it on, and that someone deserves your thanks.

To me, saying thanks is simply part of good sportsmanship. This means saying thanks to your opponent, win or lose. Without an opponent, you can't have a match or game or meet.

This also means for the child to write thank-you notes now and again to her coach or teacher or mentor.

It's also important to instill an awareness and gratitude for parental contributions. The mother can suggest, "Johnny, why don't you thank Dad for driving you to the meet." The father can ask, "Mary, did you remember to thank Mom for helping you with your science project?" Kids need reminding and, hopefully, it will eventually become a habit. Children must be encouraged to be as considerate of their parents as they are of everyone else in their lives who lends a helping hand.

However, don't expect your child to appreciate and thank you for all you do to help them pursue their Passion. You are not in this for that. You are in this with unconditional love for your child. So don't look for constant thanks and gratitude. If it comes, great, that's a wonderful bonus.

We all like praise. And not only will your child's thanks and praise make others feel better, but it will actually make them feel good. Praise is like love—the more you give out the more you seem to get in return. Saying thanks will also result in a better relationship with the coach and teacher.

Another point I'd like to make is that as a parent, don't ever be critical of your child's coach! No coach is perfect. They are only human. If your child is in high school, why should you expect to have an Olympic-caliber coach? You can't. But as your child moves up in ability, then he will get better and better coaching. Look, a college English professor is probably more knowledgeable than a grade-school teacher, and yet in truth, a fourth-grader would not be better off with a college professor. The best coach is the one that is on the right level for your child right now.

My nephew, Josh, was a star on his seventh-grade track team, winning every race in the 200 and 400 meters. When I went to watch a meet, he frequently was critical of his coach, saying things like, "She doesn't do this and doesn't know that."

I took Josh to breakfast the next morning and said, "Hey, buddy. I want you to tell me five things that your track coach does well. Tell me five positive things about her."

He thought and wrestled with it for a minute and then said, "Well, she isn't paid much and does spend a lot of time with us."

"Come on. What else."

"Well, she has scheduled more meets for us. She is organized. She runs the meets well. And she really does care about us and works hard with us."

"Okay, Josh. When you get home I want you to sit down and write her a note thanking her for all she did for you and the kids on that team last spring."

Josh wrote a wonderful, heartfelt note and sent it off to the coach.

I reminded him to keep that kind of thinking and attitude, and for him to be a leader and get the other members of the squad behind the coach too. When Josh returned to school in the fall the coach named him the captain of the track team. I then wrote Josh and said, "Hey buddy. What a wonderful honor and a great responsibility. You get out there and help that coach and all the other students on your team. Got it?"

"Yeah. I got it, Uncle Wayne."

To amplify on this concept, Josh had a teammate who chose to quit the squad "because of the coach." When this young man related the story to me, I replied, "You were the big loser. You didn't get to compete and be part of the track program. What did quitting accomplish?"

The next season, Josh's friend was back on the squad and behind the coach all the way.

A young athlete must also support other players on the team. A practice or rehearsal environment is much more conducive to improving when you are out there each afternoon with friends. When you are working together and helping each other and rooting for each other, good things happen. It is axiomatic that championship teams always have the magic of chemistry. Chemistry starts with one player supporting and rooting for another one. This spirit is infectious.

Coaches aren't the only role models in this setting. Just as your child looks up to a player three years older, someone three years younger may look up to your child. So have your child help and encourage them. By helping others your child is also helping himself.

In our junior tennis program of about 85 players, the older kids always helped the younger kids. In that way the older ones got a sense of giving back, while the younger ones idolized the older players and benefited from their example. They were like a bunch of cousins and it really helped our program grow.

The same with opponents. Make friends with your opponents. Congratulate them after a victory or tell them "tough luck" following a loss. Don't treat them as enemies. Remember, without someone across the net—or guarding you on the basketball court—you don't have a game.

Speaking of winning and losing, you as a parent must emphasize that good sportsmanship is more important than winning. Let your child know that cheating is unacceptable and there is no excuse for boorish behavior. I have seen many parents come down harder on the child for their poor behavior when they lose, but tend to overlook it when the youngster wins. As a parent, be steadfast when it comes to demanding good sportsmanship, at all times, win or lose.

My wife, Kathy, took Mike and Bob to a local tournament at the Oakridge Athletic Club in Simi Valley when they were eight. While Mike was playing his singles match, he was displaying some very unsportsmanlike behavior. When he missed a shot, he would slam down his racket in disgust. He also made a few disrespectful comments to the umpire and was churlish to his opponent.

Kathy waited until he was winning the match and then calmly walked out on the court and told Mike to pack up his racket because he was defaulting the match. Mike was shocked and in disbelief. She then calmly and silently drove Mike around the block from the tournament site and stopped the car.

Mike was in tears: "I was winning that match, Mom."

"I want you to know right now, Mike," Kathy replied, "it is far more important to me who you are as a person than who you ever will be as a tennis player. If the only way you can win is to be a bad sport, then we're stopping it all right here."

Mike pleaded with his mom to give him another chance, so after going back to the tournament and apologizing to the tournament director, the umpire and his opponent, he was allowed to play in the doubles with his brother.

Did Kathy make her point? Well, years later, Mike and Bob went on to win the Southern California Junior Sportsmanship Award in 1996.

Bjorn Borg has always been known in the tennis world as a great sportsman, but it wasn't always so. Once, as a junior, he had a racket-throwing episode. His dad promptly took away the young Swede's racket for a full month. Not only did Bjorn go on to become a record-setting champion, but his behavior was always impeccable.

Finally, as a parent you must always display good sportsmanship. Remember that children often learn more from what you do than from what you say. You can't ask for good behavior from your child, and then go yell at an official or another parent. It's tough to resist sometimes, but always take the high road. Don't let your emotions run away from you on the champion's path. Remember, your child is watching and learning from you.

CHAPTER 13

Champions Aim for Straight A's

The guy who won't do his homework misses the free throws at the end.

—Larry Bird

*I*t is vital for your child to be an excellent student. He can't be sloppy in academics and then also be a true champion in his Passion. They both go together.

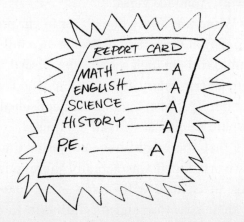

I do not worship at the altar of high IQ as the key to good grades any more than I think that great athletic ability will automatically make you a champion. Nor do I think that musical talent is genetically programmed into our DNA. I think it is the child with Passion and a sound Daily Schedule who pursues his dreams in a diligent and organized way who becomes a success and a champion. If she listens in class, does the homework each night, does the required reading and studies for those tests, she'll get straight A's, or close to it.

I believe if you follow the Formula, which includes scheduling two hours each day for homework and getting rid of your TV and video games, any child can—and should!—get excellent grades.

I also believe doing so is of the utmost importance. Excellence breeds excellence. The same tools that serve a child in schoolwork—dedication, goal setting, focus, etc.—also help the child succeed on the court or playing field or track or stage. If you are a champion in the classroom, you have a better chance of being a champion outside the classroom as well. And vice versa.

Molly White was a very fine player in our program who went on to play at University of Pacific on a full-ride tennis scholarship. While in high school, she missed most of one year due to an arm injury and wasn't able to keep up with her daily tennis regimen and tournament schedule.

You would think that with all the time she now had on her hands that she would have an easier time with her academic work, but it was actually the opposite. I have found this to be true with many other players. When they lost their structure and discipline in their Passion, they squandered their time. They found that the more time they had, the more time they wasted. Interestingly, they also had lost the confidence and self-esteem that their Passion provided which had also helped them in the classroom. Like I said, excellence breeds excellence.

The great football coach Vince Lombardi said, "Winning is a habit." Well, getting good grades is a habit too. Your child must not only spend two hours studying every day, he should do it at the same time and in the same place. This creates a positive habit. And positive habits create success.

As a parent, it is one of your roles and duties to help your child be organized and to study diligently. You must also take an interest in each and every subject he studies. The same rules work with academics as with athletics and the arts. In short, make it Fun. Display your own love for learning and they will take cues from you.

Indeed, you must find a way to make Fun permeate their studies. This means taking your child to a California mission when they are studying the early history of the state. It means going to the Getty Museum and the Gettysburg battlefield and to the tidal pools. You get the point.

Besides traveling for educational field trips, I believe it's all right to occasionally miss school to attend motivational events. And if you follow the Formula, your child will be getting great grades, so you are not shortchanging school. You are, in fact, enhancing it.

Taking school children to see a Stanford vs. University of Georgia tennis match not only gets them fired up about tennis, but also will make them want to go to college. They'll see a beautiful campus with vibrant young people everywhere. They'll know what college is about and it will help make their dreams take shape. They will actually see their dreams in action.

Sadly, I often hear of parents and teachers not allowing youngsters to have these inspirational and enriching experiences because "they can't miss a day of school." I disagree. I say champions miss a school day now and then for a good reason.

A few years ago I spoke to 300 coaches in a large banquet room in Chicago. I asked them early in my talk how many of them had taken their players to see the NCAA Tennis Championships that had been recently held at nearby Notre Dame. I was shocked and dismayed when I saw only three hands go up.

Then one veteran coach remarked from the audience, "Of course we couldn't because we didn't want to take the kids out of school."

"Sir," I asked, "how many youngsters in your program have gone on to play big-time college tennis in the past 20 years?"

"Well . . . none," he stammered.

"Sir, we have had over 100 players go on to play NCAA Division I college tennis precisely because we took them out of school to see matches on campuses all over Southern California. They all came back more fired up than ever to play tennis. And more important, more fired up than ever to go to college."

To conclude, your child's academics and Passion work hand in hand. They should have a symbiotic relationship.

CHAPTER 14

No TV and No Video Games

I realize now how precious each day is.

> —Basketball Coach Jim Valvano,
> as he was dying of cancer

Kathy and I didn't allow a TV in our home when Mike and Bob were growing up. To be honest, however, that might not have mattered because they were always too busy to watch TV.

No TV? That probably seems radical to you. I think it only makes perfect sense.

Every parent should know about a recent landmark study that was published in *Pediatrics* magazine, which indicates that frequent TV watching by infants and toddlers may shorten their attention span by age seven. The stimulation of watching TV, the study says, can actually "rewire" the brain of young children because of the quickly moving images on the screen. This, in turn, can affect the ability of these children to concentrate during their very important early school years as they are often more impulsive and restless than other children.

And a recent survey says American youth under age 18 watch an average of 6.2 hours of television a day—that's more than 40 hours a week! Just the commercial time alone adds up to nearly 10 hours a week. Astounding and eye-opening, isn't it?

I guarantee you that in the time spent just watching commercials, a kid could learn to become a terrific drummer or write a novel or raise his or her grades from C's to A's.

Now, let's take it further and imagine what can be accomplished if you free up all of those 40 hours most kids spend in front of the TV weekly. Think of all the books they could read—or write! Think how great a golfer they could become.

What terrific artwork they could create. Pick any Passion and the child could develop excellence in it.

It's just too easy to sit and watch some mindless show or MTV and the hours disappear with nothing accomplished and the next day you don't even remember what you watched. What a waste. That's why it's been called a TV wasteland. When you watch TV, except for a rare educational program, you take away nothing from the experience.

Now I'm not saying Mike and Bob never watched TV. They just didn't watch it in our home. If there was something really good on, something really worth watching, like a National Geographic special or a Civil War documentary or the Wimbledon finals, we would get in the car and go to a friend's home to watch it.

The thing is, this took planning. We had to call and ask if we could come over. (Special thanks to the Rettenmaiers

and the Henklemans for letting us drop in from time to time.) We had to get ready, get in the car and drive there. The message to the boys was: This is worth watching.

I can't emphasize this point enough: No TV in your house!

Okay. Now that you are getting rid of your TV, get rid of all video games too.

The cold truth is that video and computer games will rob your child of a chance to reach his or her true potential.

Indeed, numerous studies have show that playing video games is addictive. That's right: *Video Games Are Addictive.* It appears the excitement of these games causes the brain to release a chemical that causes this reaction. Symptoms of computer or video game addiction in children include:

- Most of nonschool hours are spent playing video games.
- Falling asleep in school.
- Not keeping up with assignments.
- Worsening grades.
- Lying about computer or video game use.
- Choosing to play video games, rather than see friends.
- Irritability when not playing a video game.
- Dropping out of other social groups, clubs, and sports.

Are these things you want for your child? Of course not! Most experts agree that if a youngster becomes addicted to video games, the parent needs to intervene and provide attractive alternatives. I say it's wiser to avoid the addiction problem by intervening beforehand with the attractive alternatives of a Passion and Secondary Passion.

Now, this is not to say you can't use computer games that teach a child to touch-type, for instance. Computer games for educational purposes are fine, but not for playing mindless games.

I know this sounds harsh. I know how badly kids want video games. Oh, how I know. All of Mike and Bob's young friends had video games.

"We don't have a video game," the twins would whine. "Everyone thinks we're weird. They don't want to come to our house."

I said "No" a thousand times.

After the 1,001st "No," Mike and Bob devised a plan. They drew up a list of chores, including making their beds, taking the trash out, doing the dishes, and taking a shower every day. Talk about a Daily Schedule! They said they would check off every item, every day, for a full year. In return they could get a video game.

When I still said "No," they further promised to only play it for one hour on Friday nights. If they missed just one chore on one day, the whole deal was off. I thought it was impossible to do for a week, much less an entire year. I finally said, "Okay, guys, you're on."

Guess what? They accomplished that list for an entire year!

I didn't know it at first, but they blew the "One-Hour Friday Night Rule" the very first week. Indeed, when we got that video game, it was the first time Mike and Bob ever wanted to go home from the tennis courts early. They said they had extra homework.

This went on for about a month. Playing tennis went from being their No.1 Crazy Passion to ranking behind video games. Music, their Secondary Passion, fell to third. In fact, they were playing zero music. And they weren't spending as much time on their homework, either.

Well, I typed up a speech to the kids. "Guys, let's remember your dreams," I said and showed them the list of their goals. "You can be tennis champions, great musicians, and get straight A's, but in the past month you have started heading for mediocrity." I went on for 15 minutes giving them my most Motivational and positive speech ever.

Their response was, "Okay, Pop."

I took the video game and threw it into the barranca behind our home. It is still down there rusting to this day.

Never forget the power of video games and TV. They will override the Formula.

CHAPTER 15

Champions Say "No" to Cigarettes, Alcohol, and Drugs

Ten enemies cannot hurt a man as much as he can hurt himself.

—Buddha

*Y*our child must not smoke, drink or take drugs.

It is vitally important that you talk about these destructive forces with your child. Talk with them early and talk with them often. Give them a rational discussion about people who have ruined their lives, or even died, because of drugs and alcohol. Explain the biology of what these chemicals do to your body and brain. Discuss the harmful effects on performance and overall health.

I've never met a person whose life has been enhanced by smoking, drinking or taking drugs. In fact, I have seen many lives ruined and cut short by these three.

My approach and belief here is not religious or moral. It is simply this: These things don't work with your child's Passion. My contention is that kids who follow the Formula never even get into these terrible things in the first place. They flat-out don't have time for them and thus aren't constantly exposed to them.

Also, I have seen that kids who are successful, who are budding champions, are held in such high esteem by others that their peers do not try to bring them down by pressuring them to drink and use drugs.

I used to tell the juniors in our tennis program, "You'll never become a smoker or an alcoholic if you never have one cigarette or that first drink. Make your line of defense out front. Just don't ever get started or even go there. And don't 'hang' with people who do."

Finally, and most important, if you want to be a great parent—and obviously you do or you wouldn't be reading this book—set a good example! Kids learn from what their parents do rather than what we say!

Show your child what your values are, and they will become your child's values. Don't waste your time, and your child's time, by lecturing. Spend your time setting a positive example.

I mean, you can't tell your child to be honest and then brag about cheating on your taxes. You can't expect your child to "control his temper" if you lose your temper in front of him.

If you tell your child to respect others and to treat a referee the same way you treat a bank president or the No. 1 tennis player in the world, then you can't show a lack of respect to a waitress or coach or neighbor. Your words will ring hollow. Through your hypocritical actions you will have lost your child's trust. And without trust, forget it, the Formula won't work.

Don't underestimate the influence your actions and values have on your child. They will mirror what they see you do, so make sure they see you do positive things.

This includes letting them see you do charitable deeds. My co-author Woody Woodburn began a Holiday Ball Drive a few years ago to collect new sports balls from readers of his newspaper column to give to underprivileged children. In the past four years this has added up to more than 1,900 new balls—and 1,900 smiles.

But that's not all. Seeing this, Woody's daughter, Dallas, started a holiday drive of her own and in the past two Christmases has collected and distributed a total of more than . . . drum roll, please . . . 5,000 new books to needy children!

I am so proud of Dallas, just as I am of Mike and Bob who do more free junior tennis clinics than any pros on the ATP Tour, including charity events for The Washington Tennis & Education Foundation; the Tim & Tom Gullikson Foundation for Brain Tumor Research and Prevention and Support; the Elton John Aids Foundation; the UCSB Tennis Teams; the Cal Poly Tennis Teams; the Ventura County Junior Tennis Patrons; the Santa Barbara Tennis Patrons; the Andre Agassi Foundation; the Andy Roddick Foundation; WECANN for Abused Children; and donate money to a dozen other charities.

Kids look up to superstar athletes and rock stars, but these are secondary role models. A parent is not only a child's first role model, but also a child's most important role model. Therefore, setting a good example, in all ways, is a huge priority as a parent!

CHAPTER 16

Tough Times

Many a tear has to fall, but it's all in the game,
all in the wonderful game.

—Sung by Tommy Edwards

I can remember, and more than once, standing with Mike and Bob beneath some stadium bleachers after a tough loss when the tears fell. Losing and heartbreak, like the song says, are all in the game.

It's wise to remember what renowned teaching pro Vic Braden points out: On any given day, half of the tennis players in the world walk off the court losers. It's the same in football, basketball and baseball—half the competitors win and the other half lose.

There's even more disappointment in the performing arts where 100 might try out for a part or gig that can only go to one winner.

Indeed, there are going to be ups and downs along the sojourn to becoming a champion. Real big ups and huge downs. As John Wooden says, "For every peak, there's a valley."

"It's a roller-coaster ride," says my pal Dick Leach, the respected former coach of the USC men's tennis team—and wonderful dad to champions Ricky and Jon.

Some days you'll feel like you are on top of the Matterhorn while other days (and weeks!) it'll seem like you and your child are at the bottom of the Grand Canyon or California's infamous Death Valley and you can't imagine ever climbing back to the top.

In other words, tears will fall. There will be upset stomachs and headaches and heartaches.

The disappointment will come in many forms. Your young star basketball player will find herself on the second string and on the bench. Your daughter, a wonderful singer, talented dancer and gifted actress gets passed over for the lead in the junior high school musical. Your son, the next Andre Agassi, loses to a kid who just bunts the ball over the net. Maybe your son the quarterback throws an interception that is returned for the game-winning touchdown.

What do you do when such disasters strike? And make no mistake, the disasters will come knocking on your child's door.

At tough times, remember to provide Perspective. You provide Perspective by explaining how losing is, as Tommy Edwards sang, in the early 60s, " . . . all in the game. All in the wonderful game."

When your child loses a very tough game or match or tryout, you provide Perspective by telling her about the time you lost a match you felt you should have won, or made a mistake that cost your team the contest. Remind him about the school elections you lost. The tests you failed. The part in the play you didn't get. The time your voice cracked or you forgot the chord progression.

In fact, tell your child about the business deal that didn't go your way or the award at work that you got beaten out for. Show her that you know what she's feeling because you've not only been there, you still go through similar disappointments from time to time.

It is important to also let your child know that the pain won't last long. Let him go take a shower and have a good meal. I suggest pizza, of course, because it's hard not to have Fun at a pizza parlor. More often than not, I think you'll find that by the time you drive back home your child will have already rebounded from the loss emotionally.

For those super tough losses and really big disappointments, however, the recovery time may be a few days. Perhaps even a week or until the next contest. After a tough loss, Mike and Bob could never wait until their next match. That's one reason why it's important for your young champion to have a full schedule of athletic contests (or plays or recitals, etc.). Instead of brooding over what just happened, it puts their mind on what's coming up next.

It's impossible for a kid who has been on the planet for 8 or 10 or 12 years to have the perspective that you do after being here for 25 or 30 or 50 years. It is your role to share your experiences and perspective.

You do this through both your words and your deeds. Don't seem down yourself because your child will feed off this. Larry Meister, the affable General Manager at Barber Ford in Ventura, always told his employees, "Act enthusiastic and you'll be enthusiastic." It is true.

The reverse is also true: if you act upset or overly disappointed, your child will surely be upset and overly disappointed. So act upbeat and positive during the trying times and your child will get through the painful period easier and swifter.

Kids are resilient and recover pretty darn quickly if we just back off a little and let them. Indeed, one of the worst things you can do is to smother your child with sympathy after a loss or disappointment. It's far better to let kids hang around with their friends.

Another way to show the child perspective is to ask him/her, "What makes (fill-in-your-Passion-here) great?"

Have the child answer: "I think golf is great because . . . I think running cross country is great because . . . I think playing the drums is great because . . ."

And help the child come up with answers. For example, "I personally think tennis is great because you can play it your entire lifetime; size does not matter; boys and girls can play together; it is great exercise; you can make friends" and so on.

Then remind the child now and again of these positive things. Post them on your refrigerator.

Also, remind yourself as a parent of the big picture. Playing a sport isn't just about earning a college scholarship, it is about the Fun enjoyed and the life lessons—setting goals, learning to be dedicated, learning to overcome obstacles, learning about teamwork, fair play and good sportsmanship—along the journey.

You further provide Perspective by explaining that without valleys there would be no mountains. It's the losses that make the wins sweeter. And the tough losses make the hard-fought wins extra sweet. Without losses, it wouldn't be competition.

There is a great "Twilight Zone" TV episode from the late 1950s where a punk mobster dies and his guide in the afterlife takes him to a gambling casino where he wins at everything. He wins at craps. He hits "21" in blackjack every time. He wins at roulette. Over and over. Win, win, win.

Three months later, the guy is totally bored and totally despondent. When the dealer says, "You win again!" the punk mobster looks away and says, "Yeah, yeah, yeah. I know."

When the guide comes back on the scene, the former mobster says, "Please, please, I need some excitement. I need some ups and downs. I need to lose sometimes. Can you take me to the 'other place?'"

And the guide pauses for a long time and then intones softly, "You are in the 'other place.'"

Not only do you need lows to appreciate and enjoy the highs, you need losses because you learn more from these setbacks than you ever can from wins. After getting knocked flat on his back, the champion, with help from the coach or parent, learns to dust himself off and get right back up more focused and determined than ever. As my dad always says, "Don't let defeat make you bitter, let it make you better."

Tough losses happen to everyone. Every athlete is covered with "loss scars." No athlete, no matter how great, ever wins them all. The truth is, you'd be surprised how many loss scars superstars have. Michael Jordan, arguably the greatest basketball player ever, was cut from his high school team! Joe Montana was seventh string—that's right, seventh string—at Notre Dame but kept plugging away until he became a legend.

The pro champions lost at the junior level. They lost at the collegiate level. And they lose at the pro level.

And you know what, losing never gets any easier. Each loss is painful. Very painful. No one likes to lose, but champions hate to lose. At the same time, true champions know the pain, and falling tears, are the price of admission. Yes, it's all in the game.

Let me share a dinner conversation Kathy and I had at the home of Gary and Layne Cuoco, two of the finest parents I have ever known. Their young daughter Kaley is a wonderful kid and an "actress champion" who has been in movies with Denzel Washington and Russell Crowe, and is currently starring in the popular ABC sitcom "8 Simple Rules." She has also made TV commercials as well as modeled in print ads.

All of this and Kaley still found time to compete on the junior tennis circuit as a nationally ranked player. Oh, yes, and you should hear her jam on the drums. Meanwhile, Kaley's younger sister, Bre, is an accomplished dancer and a beautiful singer.

I asked Gary, "Has Kaley, who seems to go from one commercial to a movie to a commercial to a TV show and back to a movie, ever had a dry spell? Has she ever gone a while and had nothing going?"

Gary replied, "Are you kidding? Dry spells happen all the time. In fact, one time Kaley went one entire year with absolutely no parts at all. She drove down to 50 straight interviews and got zilch. That's a three-hour round trip from Camarillo to L.A. or Hollywood each time."

Kaley didn't give up on her dream or lose her Passion. She did what champions do—she kept after it. She knew what my mom always says: "The darkest hour is just before dawn."

Kaley's darkest hour ended and now she's enjoying the sunshine again. She has more show business gigs than she can almost handle. But when the dry spells arrive again, and they will, she can draw on the patience and perspective she has now gained.

Learning to lose is a great life lesson. I truly believe that learning to lose with class is more important than learning to win graciously. Let's face it, being a "good winner" is easy. Being a "good loser" is hard and takes real character.

As a parent, you must be a good loser too. By this I mean take pride in your child when she loses an athletic contest but is gracious to the victor. By doing that, your child is a true champion.

Tell your child how proud you are when he sets a personal best time in a race, no matter what place he finishes. Tell him you are proud when he tries his very hardest, no matter the outcome. Maybe the opponent was too big or too fast or simply too good. The final score isn't the only measure of success.

Recording results on the refrigerator door can also help give your child a sense of perspective. Let's say Little Jake has 37 wins for the year and 22 losses. Even if he loses his next match, he can still see that he's won 37.

He can also see that he's played 60 matches overall this

year, which makes him realize that his next match isn't The Most Important Match Ever because it's just one of 61!

Similarly, when little Tanya the soccer player says, "I never score." She can look at the refrigerator and see how wrong she is because a chart there shows she has 8 goals this season and 24 over the past four years!

And when Aubrey doesn't get the part in the junior high school musical, she can look on the refrigerator and see that she has given six recitals, been in two musicals, two school band performances, and sung three solos at church in the past eight months.

That gives perspective back.

In addition to looking back for perspective, you also want your child to have perspective looking forward. How do you achieve that?

You have your youngster type on their computer their upcoming schedule of tournaments, games, tryouts, performances, track meets, writing contests, or events for whatever their Passion is. This always gives them something to work towards and look forward to rather than perhaps looking backwards and dwelling on a defeat or heartbreak.

Also, try to plan mini-vacations during your child's competitions. Kathy was great at making sure we did this. We saw the historical sites, museums, parks and hiking trails. We saw the Alamo, the Everglades, Joshua Tree National Park, Henry Clay's house, Lincoln's home, the Potomac and the Mississippi.

By combining competition and family outings you make sure that the whole experience is Fun, educational, and rewarding, and not just based on a win or loss. It gives balance and perspective.

Last, but certainly not least important, before your child goes out on the court or field, or the stage or casting room, always wish them well and tell them to be sure to have Fun.

And be sure to tell them—and often!—that you love them no matter what, and winning or losing will never change that. After all, the tough times shall pass, but your love is unconditional and forever.

CHAPTER 17

A Secondary Passion

Mens sana in corpore sano.
A Sound Mind in a Sound Body.
>—Hawthorne High School motto

Developing a Secondary Passion is a great help in dealing with those tough times. What is a Secondary Passion? Let me illustrate with a story.

Kaley Cuoco, our young actress friend who has been doing print work, commercials, TV and movies for most of her life, is also an accomplished tennis player who competes on the sectional and national level. Her Primary Passion is acting where the vast majority of her time and efforts are spent. Acting is always her top priority. However, when she isn't auditioning or acting on the set, she drives to the Mark Weil Tennis Academy for tennis clinics and to play practice matches. When her acting schedule allows, Kaley competes in tennis tournaments on the weekends.

I remember one time when Kaley was battling her guts out in a close match in Anaheim. Unfortunately, she wasn't

able to win the match. But when she came off the court, her mother greeted her with the news that she had just received a call on her cell phone from Kaley's acting agent. The sitcom that she co-stars in, "8 Simple Rules", had been picked up by ABC for the upcoming season.

Do you think Kaley was mourning over her tennis loss? No, she was too busy screaming with delight about the call from ABC. Of course, there have been many times when Kaley didn't get "call-backs" after auditions for parts and rejection was assuaged by a few big wins on the tennis court.

A Secondary Passion is more than a hobby but not so consuming as the top priority, the Primary Passion. There is definitely a desire to excel and strive for excellence, but at the same time it reduces the pressures of the main focus.

Ideally, the Secondary Passion is a counterbalance to the Primary Passion, a way to use the opposite side of the brain.

If your child's Primary Passion is in the arts, the ideal Secondary Passion would be in athletics, such as Kaley's Primary Passion, acting, and Secondary Passion, tennis. One passion is physical and the other is creative, so the energies compliment, not drain, each other.

Mike and Bob have the opposite situation. Their Primary Passion is in athletics, tennis, and their Secondary Passion is in music—the keyboard and drums. There have been times when Mike and Bob have had heart-breaking losses on the court but had a music gig that same night where they were soon smiling and laughing and having the time of their lives. The gig put the tennis loss in perspective and put a salve on their wounds, helping Mike and Bob to rebound faster and be ready to compete another day. Their identity and self-worth aren't completely riding on their tennis results because they know they have talents in other areas, too.

Believe me, Mike and Bob are not unique in combining sports and music as Primary and Secondary Passions. To give you an idea, Detroit Lions standout quarterback Joey Harrington began banging the keyboards at age 4 and his mother soon enrolled him in classical and jazz classes. The steps of progression later had Joey getting instruction from the likes of famous jazz pianist Gordon Lee and George Mitchell, Diana Ross's keyboardist for 20 years. Long after his NFL career is over, Harrington will still be making music.

Same with San Diego Chargers legendary passer Doug Flutie, who is an accomplished drummer and plays numerous gigs with The Flutie Gang Band.

And then there was Hall of Fame quarterback Otto Graham, who grew up playing the piano, violin, cornet and French horn. In fact, at age 16 Graham was the Illinois state champion in the French horn.

It's not just a quarterback thing either, this mixing of music and sports. New York Yankees star outfielder Bernie Williams is also an accomplished guitarist and composer who has released a CD titled "The Journey Within" which is a melodic, contemporary, and Latin flavored jazz album.

It also works the other way. Before he became a world famous rock star, Rod Stewart dabbled with his secondary passion and briefly played professional soccer.

Boyd Tinsley, gifted violinist for The Dave Matthews Band—Mike and Bob's favorite group, by the way—has a Secondary Passion for playing tennis.

Believe me, he's pretty darn good with these strings, too!

I could go on and on, but you get the idea: music and sports compliment each other beautifully as Primary and Secondary Passions.

Having a Secondary Passion is not taking your child to piano on Monday, tennis on Tuesday, soccer on Wednesday, and dance on Thursday. It's tempting for parents to overschedule and overexpose their child to too many activities. You may mean well, but there is a finite amount of energy, time, and focus that any child can muster. To be a champion in a field of endeavor takes consistent effort and determination. Too many activities and there can be no Primary Passion, much less a Secondary Passion.

I find myself in total agreement with Arnold Patent who wrote in *You Can Have It All: A Simple Guide to a Joyful and Abundant Life*:

> *You want to start with just one activity. This relates to the efficient use of energy. The more you focus your energy on one activity, the more power that activity will have. Once you achieve success with one activity, you can move on to another.*
>
> *There are many multitalented people. The ones who are the most successful are the ones who started by focusing their attention on one talent and then went on to focus on another. By giving just a little of our attention to several activities, we scatter our energy and make it almost impossible to enjoy any of our talents at any real level of success. The dilettante syndrome is well-known.*
>
> *If you look at the life of a recognized superstar, you will notice that most of the things the superstar does are very ordinary. He or she is perceived as a superstar for expressing one talent in an outstanding way.*

I believe we each have the natural ability to express at least one talent on a high level.

CHAPTER 18

Love Must Be Unconditional

Love is never lost.

—Washington Irving

Your child does not earn love by winning or practicing or singing well or painting a masterpiece. Your love must be unconditional at all times or else you run the risk of losing their trust. And the Formula will not work without trust and unconditional love.

It is vital to show your love to your child whether he wins a match or loses. Show as much love whether she wins a talent show or forgets her song midway through the performance. Whether he gets A's and B's, or C's. Whether she is a star athlete or a bench-warmer; the star of the play or a stagehand.

The last thing you want is for your child to equate winning, or performing well or succeeding, with love. The trick is to show no more love after a win, no less love after a defeat. In fact, if anything, you must be more low-key after a victory and show more love following a loss because

your child will be down and need you to help pick him up emotionally.

Okay, so what should you say after a win or loss? I have made it easy for you by scripting your proper response for both occasions. And both should be the same.

My script, win or lose:

First, let your child come to you. Neither parent should go rushing up to the child. He will come to you when he is ready. This is as true after a win as after a loss. After a win, hold back and let others congratulate the child first. Remember, this is her gig, not yours. You say you want to share her glory? No! Let her friends go up to her and share her moment.

After your child does come up to you, here is what you say, win or lose: "Would you like some water? Or would you rather have Gatorade?"

Then ask: "What do you want to eat—Chinese, Mexican, Italian or McDonald's?"

Finally, ask: "Do you want to drive or want me to?" (If the child is under 16, skip this question and you drive.)

It's really that simple. If the child wants to talk about the match, you listen. But don't critique. No legal-pad reviews. Never be overbearing. Remember, the more unconditional the love, the better for the child. This means showing your child support and understanding at all times and in every way. This means to be small!

Being small means to not put big pressure on the child. Your role is to minimize pressure, not create it. So no legal-pad scouting reports and no big pep talks beforehand!

Before a talent show or match, what you don't want to say is: "Don't make a mistake!" That creates pressure and fear. And don't say, "Try hard" or "Give it your best effort." These are an insult to a champion. They always try hard and give their best effort.

Instead, here is what you should say before a match or performance: "I love you. Good luck. Have some fun." In others words, keep it simple. Keep it small.

Another thing, don't talk about the competition or the big event for days on end beforehand. You don't want to get the juices up too soon. When the time comes, if you have been following the Formula, the child will be ready.

How do you act during a game, match or performance? Above all, try to stay calm. Have a smile on your face, if you can. Your child will feed off your emotions.

Being small also means not upstaging your child. For example, I wanted to play the drums well so that Mike and Bob could see how to do it, but I did not step in and show them how good I was every time they tried to play something.

If your child is trying out for Pop Warner football, don't tell them you were All-American at Michigan. By making yourself big, you will make them feel small.

Come on, they are 3 feet tall—you are 5 or 6 feet. You are quite an imposing figure to them. You don't want to squelch their ability to grow by providing too much shade.

To me, being small means NEVER beating your child at anything. Not at chess, not at Monopoly, not at tennis or playing 1-on-1 basketball in the driveway. But be a good actor at losing. Don't make it obvious. Be interested in keeping it close and let the child enjoy winning.

Similarly, don't "top" them. If they are class vice president, don't point out that you were school president. If they make all-league second team, don't tell them that you were first-team.

If you give unconditional love, your child will always consider you a safe harbor to come home to in calm or rough seas.

CHAPTER 19

Become Involved and Volunteer

A man there was and they called him mad;
The more he gave, the more he had.

—John Bunyan

Please, please, please become involved with the entity or organizations involved in your child's Passion—be it a sport, or dance, or writer's guild—and help it succeed and grow. This is not only good for your child, it is good for you and above all it is good for the entity.

This means serving on the organizational board. This means helping with fund-raising drives. This means volunteering to time races at a swim meet. This means phoning in the results of a tournament, not just for your child's matches, but for all the matches.

You will not only make the sport (or art, music, whatever endeavor) better, you will help yourself and your child by learning about more opportunities. I can't tell you how much Kathy and I learned from being involved in Mike and Bob's tennis. I really enjoyed my time serving on USTA Boards, the SCTA Junior Tennis Council and ranking committees. We learned about national and regional events and endorsement opportunities, about camps and clinics and all sorts of things that we wouldn't have known about otherwise.

But more than just helping yourself and your child, I think you have a moral obligation to get involved. It's sort of like the Boy Scout adage to leave the campsite better than you found it. I can honestly, and proudly, say that when the Bryan boys left the junior ranks, junior tennis was better than when they arrived. We wrote letters, we raised money, we made donations, and we spread tennis in the community. We took kids to matches. We got the local press interested in junior tennis and helped increase attendance at high school matches.

So please, volunteer, volunteer, volunteer.

CHAPTER 20

Work with the Media and Sponsors

The time to make friends is before you need them.

—John Wooden

*T*oo many parents complain about not getting enough, or any, media coverage on their child's sport or performance.

What these same parents forget is that the media is made up of people. The press needs to know about stories "out there." If they aren't covering and writing about what you think they should, maybe they are not ignoring your sport but simply aren't aware of the stories. Let them know.

Help them. Phone in, fax in or mail in press releases with results. Make sure your press releases are neat and well written and as timely as possible. Send along pre-writes before the event and post-writes about how the event went, results, and attendance. Suggest specific times that would provide good pictures if a photographer can make it out there. Include phone numbers of people to call

for additional information. By working with the media instead of complaining, you can help your child and help the sport or organization.

And remember that everything you phone in or send in may not get in the paper. Woody, who was a sportswriter for our local paper, and I are friends, but that still didn't mean all the results and tournaments I sent in got written up. Often times space is limited.

Sometimes there isn't the manpower to write the stories or take the photographs. So be happy when you do get coverage; don't get mad when you don't; and keep trying to get coverage in the future.

When your story or results do get in the paper, or on the radio or TV, write a thank-you note. Like I said, the press are people. A lunch or dinner from time to time is also helpful. Treat the press people like you would like to be treated. Good ink doesn't come down from the sky, it comes from solid relationships and helping the local press cover your sport or musical performance or play.

Same with sponsors. Write thank-you notes. Develop a relationship. Long before Mike and Bob were getting free products, they were writing letters to companies. Like: "I love Adidas. I dream of one day wearing Adidas. Sincerely, Mike and Bob Bryan, age 11." Guess who eventually gave them a contract with free shoes and clothes?

Indeed, Mike and Bob had better sponsorship deals along the way, and do so even today, because they developed relationships early on and have maintained them. Today they even do things for their agent, like appearing at extra clinics, and you know what? It almost always ends up coming back to benefit Mike and Bob two-fold in the long run.

Think of ways to help the company. Remember at all times they are a business and are trying to be profitable. How can you help them promote their product and make more sales? Talk up their product and always hold that racket up for those photos!

It's just the basic philosophy of trying to give more than you get. Human Relations 101.

CHAPTER 21

The Glide Path Out Begins Early

The worst thing you can do for those you love is the things they could and should do for themselves.

—Abraham Lincoln

I strongly believe in sitting as far away from your child's performance, game or match as possible. Once again, it is your child's endeavor, not yours. This is even more important if you as a parent are the nervous type. They will feed off that nervousness. You reduce their pressure by every 10 feet you can move away. Binoculars are a good idea.

Look, it's not about you standing there when your child wins Wimbledon—or wins a ribbon at a science fair—with an arm around him. If he wants to put his arm around you, hey, that's pretty cool. But you want to practice being out of it. Sit back. Sit off to the side. Make your child more self-reliant.

Put your energy into Motivating and supporting them. The younger they are, the more they will need you there at an event. As they grow and progress, they will need you there in person less and less. Eventually, you will have to glide out of the picture all together so they can do their thing without you there at all. So you might as well get close to the exit now.

You want to start that smooth exit early on. This means having your child sometimes ride to tournaments or games with friends and their parents. There's nothing more Fun and Motivational and stress-reducing than to load up a group of youngsters in a van and head off for an event of some kind.

Make a point of not going to every one of your child's meets, games or performances. You don't want to have the "me and my child against the world" syndrome. Here's what I think you'll find—your child will do just as well with you there as not. However, if they only do well with you there, you have a problem to work on.

If they only do well when you aren't there, you are the problem. Fortunately, the earlier chapters in *Raising Your Child to be a Champion in Athletics, Arts, and Academics* will help you solve this problem.

CHAPTER 22

Putting the Formula into Action

Often the single most powerful action you can take
is to help people focus on what they want.

—Brian D. Biro, *Beyond Success*

*J*osh Colwell and the Drums. This is a beautiful story of how all the elements of the Formula were put into practice.

Josh Colwell is my nephew. His father Dan, my brother-in-law, passed away suddenly from a heart attack in October of 2001. Josh was only 12 at the time, and as you can imagine he took the tragic loss extremely hard.

What could I do to help this young man who lived 448 miles to the north of me in Grass Valley? I was deeply worried about the boy.

I invited Josh to come down and stay with us in Camarillo for a while, thinking that getting away might do him some good. During our visit I took Josh into our music room. Mike and Bob were home from the ATP Tour at the time, so we put on a little 20-minute jam session for Josh. I could tell that Josh was really having fun just listening.

When Mike and Bob were done playing, I said, "Hey Josh, grab these sticks and hop up on that drum stool."

In a Fun way, little by little, over the next couple of days, we played around with the drums. Josh showed frustration at first, but I persisted in making it Fun and taking him forward until finally, after a few days, he could play the basic rock'n'roll groove.

When Josh went back home to Grass Valley, I had his mom get him some drums and also instructed her to phone all over a 50-mile radius to find the most positive and most Fun drum teacher in the area. She found out about a teacher named Larry, a real cool guy who played in several bands and had a real funky drum studio about 40 minutes away in Auburn.

I went up to visit Josh a number of times, and each time I was happy to see how he was enjoying his music and I was also very proud to see how nicely he was progressing. He sounded good. I worked with him some more and then went and bought him a new cymbal which he loved. Then I asked Larry when he was playing next, and that Saturday Josh and I drove to hear him play an outdoor gig at a street fair. Larry played and sang and was flat-out awesome. He was obviously having a blast up there on the stage.

Josh certainly was having a blast watching his new teacher. You should have seen Josh's eyes—they lit up and grew as big as saucers. After the gig, Josh went up on stage

to congratulate Larry. Larry, being a great and caring mentor, gave Josh the biggest greeting you can imagine and instead of talking about his own performance, he started bragging on and on about Josh and his drumming. Talk about Motivating a student!

A couple months went by. Josh phoned me and said, "Uncle Wayne, I've put a five-piece band together with my friends. We have drums, a lead guitar player, a piano player, a rhythm guitar player and a bass player. And we stink! We can't play anything. And, uh, there's a school district talent show coming up and we want to try and qualify. The problem is the tryout is in two weeks. And, of course, we really want to win the contest but there's usually about 40 acts. Can you come up and help us?"

"I'm on my way," I answered.

To make a long story short, we spent lots of fun hours playing "Louie, Louie", the ol' Kingsmen hit from the early '60s. We practiced every note, every nuance, the fills, the leads, the rap beginning, the lighting, and the choreography.

"Choreography?" the kids asked in amazement.

"Yeah, guys, choreography."

In a short time they were amazed at how good it was sounding and often they would just burst into smiles and laughter. It was wonderful to see Josh going from liking music, to loving it. He was starting to become crazy about it. He was getting a Passion.

Josh discovered that he was a leader. He called the guys and set up rehearsals. He cleaned his garage up for a rehearsal place. He found his dad's excellent old P.A. system. Lots of kids started showing up at the practices. He invited them and lots of his other school friends to come to the big event to root on the "Manehunies". And guess what? The Manehunies went up on stage for that big talent show and stomped! They performed absolutely perfectly, blew everyone away and walked off with the grand prize of $50.

More important, Josh walked away with newfound self-esteem and a newfound Passion.

Seeing Josh up there on stage with the Manehunies was one of my proudest moments. Josh congratulated the other contestants on the microphone and also thanked the teacher who put on the talent show. I chuckled as Josh and his bandmates stood outside being interviewed by not one, but two local newspaper reporters while a photographer snapped away.

Success leads to more success, and sometimes quickly! The Manehunies were asked to play a couple of songs that same night at a huge local dance. So we had to work the rest of the day learning one more song! But it was worth it as they again rocked the place with more than 200 kids crowding the stage, rooting and cheering wildly, while the band members gave their fans high-fives.

Josh is on his way now. He says all the kids at school treat him differently. More important, Josh sees himself differently. He sees himself as a champion. He can't get the smile off his face. He lights up with pride when he watches the video tape of those first two performances by the Manehunies.

And well he should. Think of all the lessons he learned while taking his "drum journey." The power of a Passion. Organization. Teamwork. Leadership. Promotion. Goal setting. Working through difficulty. He also learned that hours and effort lead to success. And that lots of hours and lots of effort lead to big success.

Now let's look back at that story and examine the elements of the Formula that were put into action.

Side-Door Motivation: Josh sat right in the middle of the music room and watched the Bryan Bros. Band rock. He saw it, felt it and could definitely hear it. I also took Josh to watch his drum teacher's gig.

Fun: We made the initial stages of his playing the drums a contest. When all five kids in the band started rehearsing they had an absolute ball being together and practicing the song. The entire process was Fun.

Steps of Progression: Josh's drums were broken down to simple elements so he could feel successful right from the beginning. Each band member learned his music, vocal, and choreography part incrementally.

Find the Right Coach: Josh's mother made many phone calls to finally find the teacher who had enthusiasm and charisma and who emphasized performance and Fun. The teacher demonstrated his own personal Passion and joy with the drums in the studio and at the gig.

Less Is More: Josh had a little taste of drumming in our music room and then he called me to give him more.

Goal Setting: Josh and his friends' goal was to learn one song well enough to win the talent show.

Play First, Learn Later: Josh and his friends wanted to learn a song and perform before learning the intricacies of their instrument. Now that they are hooked, they will gradually learn technique.

Instill Values: Josh was encouraged to thank the teacher and talent show director and congratulate the other contestants.

You can see that the elements of the Formula are very powerful and can get results quickly. Josh is one of many success stories. Your child is ready to start his journey today!

So clear off the door of your refrigerator and unplug your TV because there's an amazing, exciting and rewarding road trip coming up. Bring your camera because you'll surely want to take some pictures. It's going to be an awesome experience and everyone who reads The Formula gets to go on this thrilling journey with their child.

As you embark on this wonderful ride, beginning today not tomorrow, let me leave you with this thought:

Make sure it is a *FUN* trip!

About the Authors

Wayne Bryan has been a teaching professional for more than thirty years. He co-owned and managed the Cabrillo Racquet Club in Camarillo, California, and has coached numerous nationally-ranked juniors. A frequent lecturer and speaker, Wayne also emcees many nationally televised tennis tournaments and has appeared as a commentator on the Tennis Channel. His twin sons, Mike and Bob, are currently ranked #1 in tennis doubles in the world and both won full-ride scholarships to Stanford University. Wayne lives with his wife, Kathy, a former professional tennis player, in Camarillo, California.

Woody Woodburn is an award-winning sports columnist for the *South Bay Daily Breeze* in Torrance, California. His awards include being inducted into The Jim Murray Memorial Foundation Journalism Hall of Fame in 2003 as well being named Best Columnist by the Associated Press News Executive Council. His work has appeared in *The Best American Sports Writing 2001* and earned Notable Sports Writing honors in the 2003 edition. In addition, he is a frequent contributor to the *Chicken Soup for the Soul* series. Woody lives with his wife and family in Ventura, California.